WHERE WISDOM COMES FROM

WHERE WISDOM COMES FROM

—

How Our Experiences Make Us Wise

By Jim Schell

LIGHTS ON PUBLISHING

TUCSON, AZ | BEND, OR

Printed in the United States of America

Library of Congress Control Number: 2020904646

First Printing, 2020

ISBN 978-0-9987925-8-3

Lights On Publishing
Bend, OR / Tucson, AZ

To Mary...

I'm wise enough to know how lucky I am.

_____

WHERE WISDOM COMES FROM

CONTENTS

INTRODUCTION

"Knowledge speaks but wisdom listens."—JIMI HENDRIX

"HI JIM," JAY SAID, SIDLING UP to my table at my favorite coffee shop. "Got a minute?"

"Sure, pull up a chair," I replied. I'd just finished an hour-long conversation with Laura on an issue related to her business.

Exit Laura. Enter Jay.

"My son graduates from college in May," Jay began, with a sigh of relief. "I'm proud of him, but he's talking about taking a sabbatical to Indonesia for six months following graduation. I'm not sure that's the best use of his time or my money. I need help in deciding what to do."

I then barrage Jay with questions, and we discuss his responses, and forty-five minutes later we have a game plan for him to pursue. The two of us do this together—mostly me asking questions and Jay providing answers.

What's going on here with Laura and Jay is that someone older and more, well, tainted by life, is helping someone younger and less tainted, solve their problems. The results of those conversations have, thanks to my 83 years on this planet, resulted in people like Laura and Jay looking to me for help in making their decisions and solving their problems. In short, they perceive me to be, well ... blush ... wise.

Just What is Wisdom, Anyway?

I define wisdom as *"the sum of the lessons learned from a lifetime of experiences."* Since all of those experiences result in stories, all one needs to do when a decision is required is to pull up a story that fits the situation, recall the wisdom that came from the story, plug it into the issue du jour, flip on the brain switch, and whammo, up pops either the right question to ask or the best solution to the problem.

Thus, the more stories we have stowed away in the recesses of our brain, the more wisdom we've accumulated. That's why *older* is usually *wiser*—no rocket science there.

After three decades of owning businesses, I've experienced essentially the same issues that Laura is experiencing in her business. As for Jay? Two of my sons took off for New Zealand after graduating from college. The stories that evolved from those events provided me a foundation for helping Laura and Jay decide, or at least think differently, about how to solve their problems.

The stories we call up at times like those don't all have to be ours, incidentally— someone else's story can be just as meaningful. We can earn our wisdom equally as well by observing or reading about what happens to others. It's the story that matters, not the people who are in it.

Wisdom Improves with Age

The coolest thing about this thing we call wisdom? The older we get, the wiser we become. Imagine that, besides wine and cigars, there's something that actually improves with age! There's not much we can say that about.

Wisdom is not to be confused with *smart*, by the way: smart is what we know, while wisdom is how we use that knowledge. Or, stated more visually, "smart is knowing *how* to use a gun, wise is knowing *when* to use it."

Here's some good news on the subject of wisdom; you don't have to be old to be wise, you just have to be more experienced. A ten-year old is wise in the eyes of a five-year old; a forty-year old is wise in the eyes of a twenty-five-year old. The good news for octogenarians like me is that we can appear to be wise to a hell of a lot of people.

I grew up in the corn state of Iowa, a middle-class kid of moderate academic achievement who made more than his share of mistakes. (Nothing you could find with a Google search, but if Mom were around, she could burn my ears). I had a super-involved mother along with a hard-working dad, and a younger sister with whom I bickered but loved. Today, I'm the father of three sons, a long-time husband twice baked, and a serial entrepreneur. Oh yes, I'm a multi-published author too; you can check out my books on my Amazon author page.

You might say I've led the kind of life that the average American can relate to, which means I'm proof positive that you don't have to be a celebrity or an academic to experience wisdom-inducing stories. This book includes a random collection of the kind of stories that have led people like Laura and Jay to perceive me as someone who can help them solve their problems.

Where Wisdom Comes From is divided into four Parts; Growing Up, Grown Up, Growing Old, and Looking Back. In life, we all (hopefully) wade through the first three Parts whether we like it or not; the fourth Part, Looking Back, is an option. Within each of those four Parts you'll find a collection of stories that have added to my own personal stash of wisdom, where they're sure to remain, safely stored, until the right situation presents itself.

Using Our Wisdom

It's one thing to be wise, it's something else to use that wisdom to better the lives of others. The sharing of our wisdom provides us with a double whammy; we not only help those we share it with, we also create a legacy that will be passed on to others by the people whose lives we impact.

For me, I've chosen to use the wisdom I've earned to help younger people solve the same problems I've solved or tried to solve. To do that, I mentor them; research shows that 75 percent of millennials want a mentor, so there's no lack of mentees I can help. Some I mentor formally (regularly scheduled monthly meetings), others informally (on call when needed), but always with the same outcome in mind: to use what I've learned to help others make better decisions and lead better lives.

What *you* do with your wisdom is up to you, of course, but wisdom is a terrible thing to waste.

And a powerful thing to share.

MY WISDOM:

"Experiences come and go, but the wisdom gained

from them lasts forever."

PART ONE

GROWING UP. 1936–1958

I don't remember much about the Great Depression, but my early life was shaped by it; we lived with only the essentials and my parents never let me forget the power of a penny. I still can remember bits and pieces of World War II, including the day when our neighborhood celebrated VE Day (May 18, 1945) with a rousing bicycle parade. I didn't take education seriously growing up, much to the chagrin of my parents, especially my mom. But I did take my parents and friends seriously, which helped make up for my academic failings. I learned from my parents and friends the power of truth, the value of hard work, and how often my mom was right and I was wrong. Or, at least, misguided.

High school grad, 1954

Mom & Dad,
circa 1933

Chris & I, at peace

Mom: The Woman with All the Answers

"Life doesn't come with a manual, it comes with a Mom." —ANONYMOUS

THINK REALLY HARD NOW, WHAT'S THE very first lesson you remember learning from your mom?

For me, it was learning the definition of a swear word. My memory is sketchy, I was six or seven at the time, but the conversation probably went something like this . . .

"Hi, Mom," I said, arriving home after school. I closed the front door quietly behind me; you didn't bang doors in our house.

"Hi, honey. How was school today?" Mom asked, looking up from braiding my little sister Chris's hair.

"Uh, OK," I'm sure I replied, because that's how most kids respond to that question.

"What did you learn today?"

"Mom, what's a fart?"

"W-w-what's a what?"

"A fart?"

"Why do you want to know, honey?"

"Because Whistler is one."

And then my mother's light must have gone on, because I remember her putting her hands on her hips, straightening the bun on the back of her head, and giving me her translation of what the word "fart" meant.

"An explosion from the rear end," she probably explained, and drawing from personal experience, I knew exactly what she was talking about.

Whistler, you see, was our neighborhood pharmacist, conducting his business across the street from the grade school I attended. Someone, perhaps a visionary kid destined for bigger and better days in Los Angeles, had hand-painted in white *"Whistler is a fart"* on the wall of his red brick building.

It's funny that the meaning of a swear word is the first lesson I remember learning from my mom. What makes it so funny—and why I probably remember it—is that I learned the meaning of the word from the snow-white lips of my mother, a farmer's daughter extraordinaire and lifelong abstainer where four-letter words were concerned.

Once Mom had finished defining the word, that wasn't enough, however.

"How come you know that word, Mom?" I remember asking.

"It's part of my job, honey," she said, putting the final touches on Chris's hair. Then she patted me on the head, put on her apron, and disappeared into the kitchen.

MY WISDOM:

"The older I get the more I realize that I learned

more from my mom then I did from anyone else

in my life."

A Boy, a Dog, and a Future Career

"Every puppy should have a boy." —ANONYMOUS

IT'S SUMMERTIME, 1950. SCHOOL WAS OUT and my energy was in long supply, which means Mom's patience was in short supply, so she decided I needed something to keep me busy. An attention distracter. A chore generator.

She decided I needed a dog.

Arrangements were made and, as usual, delegated to Dad.

Well, Dad may have been in charge of the dog's delivery, but I'd bet my Rawlings baseball glove that he didn't have anything to do with its selection. The dog wasn't a poodle, but he *was* one of those pint-sized, yipper-ish fu-fu dogs that Zsa Zsa Gabor might have owned. You know the type . . . lap sitting, face licking, people-food snarfing, half baby, half dog. He was officially a Belgian Schipperke and his pedigreed name (yes, he had one of those) was Jacque de something-or-other. I called him Jack.

Several weeks following Jack's arrival, Des Moines was suffering through yet another sweltering, muggy Iowa afternoon, too hot to stay in the house. I told Mom I was heading for Waveland golf course a block away, where I'd rat (hunt for) a few golf balls, catch an evening breeze, and put a fitting end to a fine summer day.

"Take Jack with you," Mom said, handing me the leash.

Ball hunting was slow; an hour went by and I'd found one lousy golf ball. Bored and tired of towing the leashed Jack, I pulled up on a grassy slope alongside the sixth tee and hunkered down for some serious cloud gazing. Out of my pocket came that one lousy golf ball. Maybe Jack was a retriever in his prior life, so I took off his leash and gave the ball a heave.

And Jack went after that ball like it was a piece of red meat. A four-legged shortstop was what he was—without breaking stride he scooped up the ball and was back in my face before I could blink an eye. Depositing the ball at my feet, he stepped back, cocked his head, and begged for more. (If you've ever owned a dog, you know the look).

So, I gave the ball another heave. And then another. And still another. And Jack couldn't get enough, and soon he was panting and dripping saliva and making me wonder how long it would be before he gave up.

However, my patience ran out before Jack's resolve did, so I decided to give him the old fool-the-dumb-dog-with-a-fake-throw trick. You know how it works; you pretend to give the ball a toss, stuff it in your pocket, and then crack up while the dog goes nuts. Works every time.

And Jack did exactly what dogs are supposed to do, except that, after a quick search for the missing ball in the short grass of the fairway, he made a beeline for the long grass in the rough. Within seconds he was back, tail wagging, tongue panting, saliva dripping.

With a golf ball in his mouth.

Well, getting an A in Latin class couldn't have been a bigger surprise. Jack suddenly became a furry gold mine for me; a four-legged, radar-nosed, golf ball-uncovering, money machine. What's more, he loved his job, worked for peanuts, and never called in sick.

Formerly the laughingstock of my golf ball ratting friends, I now had Jack as my meal ticket. I could sell most of the balls he found and, when I'd sneak onto the course around dusk, I'd play golf with new balls instead of the old beaters I used previously. Suddenly, I was the richest kid on the block and Jack was my business partner.

Success is fleeting and, in a sad-but-true postscript, the following spring Jack made a successful charge at the postman, a charge that was successful for Jack, at least in the short term, but not so good for the postman. This resulted in Mom determining that Jack needed to be dispatched to places unknown.

I voiced fervent objections to Jack's fate and Mom's response was "Honey, remember when we first brought Jack home and you had no use for him? He was too . . . too . . . foo foo a dog for you. Do you remember?"

I studied the treads on my Converse sneakers.

"Well, Jack hasn't changed, he's still a dog and he's still foo foo, wouldn't you agree?"

I reluctantly nodded, I had an inkling of where this discussion was going.

"So, you see," she said, her eyes boring into mine, "you suddenly are fond of Jack because he's making money for you. Same dog, new perspective."

"Hmmm," I groused, realizing that, as usual, she was right.

Jack was my first introduction to Economics 101 and the career of entrepreneurship. And Mom was my first consultant.

MY WISDOM:

"Since dogs can help you learn which career you should follow is just another reason why every kid should have a dog."

Be Careful Where You Drop the F-Bomb

"Under certain circumstances, urgent circumstances, desperate circumstances, profanity provides a relief denied even to prayer." —MARK TWAIN

WHAT A KID DOES WHEN HE isn't in school depends on where that kid lives. Hawaii? He surfs. Canada? He skates. Iowa? He does what the time of year dictates. For me it was basketball in the winter, baseball in the spring, golf in the summer, and football in the fall. Iowa kids, like most of those who live in landlocked states, are Jacks of all sports and masters of none. That was me anyway.

In addition to the seasonal stuff, my friends and I played tennis, skated (I had black figure skates), tried skiing (difficult to do in a state whose topography resembles a pancake), fished, and made up a few sports of our own.

And we played ping pong. Boy did we ever, as if our life depended on it.

I had a ping pong table in my basement and my friend Dunk didn't, so he was a frequent visitor to our house. Well, he *was* a frequent visitor, that is, until something happened between him and my mom. Dunk's nickname had nothing to do with what he could do with a basketball and everything to do with his last name being Duncan. He and I were serious ping pong adversaries at the time when his shit hit Mom's fan.

You see, Mom kept a chalkboard on the wall beside the back door to our house. That chalkboard was her circa-1950 version of a to-do list; during the day, she'd stop by the chalkboard and keep track of all the stuff she needed to get done: buy milk, take Chris to music lessons, ground me; or whatever other motherly stuff that needed attending to. When it came time to run her errands, Mom would check the chalkboard and make sure that whatever was on it was being attended to. Nothing fell through the cracks in our house.

It's summertime, 1948, I'm a soon-to-be sixth grader. Mom was out of the house, running her errands and checking off the stuff on her to-do list. Dunk and I were in our basement, beating each other's brain's out in yet another life-or-death ping pong match. The game raged back and forth until finally, thanks to a valiant finish on my part, I won the third game. Game, set, and match, two games to one.

Well, Dunk was pissed about the outcome. Wait, did I say pissed? Try ballistic. As in foaming at the mouth.

So, he stomped up the stairs, spotted Mom's now-wiped-clean chalkboard, and left me a love note . . .

Fuck you Schell, it said.

Then, feeling vindicated, he tromped out the door and almost ran over Mom who was returning home from running errands.

"Hi Randy," Mom said. She always liked Dunk.

Whereupon she walked in the door, turned to her magic chalkboard and there it was, Dunk's love note, for all the world to see.

And that would be it for Dunk around our house. Hasta la vista, Mom might have said, if it had happened forty years later.

The thing is, you rarely heard the F-word back in the 40's and 50's. Oh, the high school kids would drop it in the heat of a football game, but they'd never say it in front of grownups. Dad would mutter a "hell" or a "damn" every now and then on the golf course, but if he used one at home, he'd have to put a quarter in the Swear Box that Mom maintained. Twenty-five cents was real money back in those days and could, by itself, buy a chocolate malt or a vanilla milk shake. Imagine.

Anyway, the F-Word was a rarity in those days. As a result, it was the granddaddy of all swear words, which meant that from that day forward, Dunk would be forever on Mom's shit list. Never mind that he'd go on to be an All-American football player in college and a respected Des Moines attorney until his death. Not to mention a good man, husband, and father.

Dunk and Mom have moved on to that place where we all eventually end up. But I sure hope they run into each other up there. They really oughta be friends.

MY WISDOM:

"'It's OK if my kids and their friends swear around

my house,' no mother ever said."

When a Boy's Dream Comes True

"Saddle your dreams before you ride 'em."
—MARY WEBB

IT'S 1949, AND I'M IN EIGHTH grade and a member of a basketball team that played in the Des Moines YMCA league. I'm five foot three inches tall, which makes me the smallest kid on our team. As if my shrimpiness isn't enough, I can't run, jump, or play good defense, but I can shoot a tick off a chipmunk at twenty paces with both eyes closed, so I'm the backup guard on a team where backup guards get about the same opportunities as Vice Presidents.

Some farsighted thinker, probably some unhappy short guy in the YMCA's front office, determined that us pint-sized kids were being discriminated against, so he decided to rearrange things: he created two basketball leagues, one for the tall guys and one for us short kids. And, lo and behold, the Giant League and the Midget League were born. (Those were the days before political correctness).

Well, I'll bet you can't guess where they established the cutoff height? Yep, five-foot three inches, right on the nose. Which meant I was now a giant in the Midget League. I went from Pee Wee Herman to Shaquille O'Neal overnight as the biggest kid on that team. It was a glorious reversal in an aspiring basketball player's dream.

Along with my newfound height advantage came a previously only dreamed-about role on my team. I now played the center position (where the Shaquille O'Neals of the world play), which means my teammates were looking for me when they brought the ball down the floor, as opposed to me looking for them.

As if that newfound perspective wasn't enough, when my team huddled during timeouts, it was my sweat dripping on someone else's head, not someone else's dripping on mine. Following the game, the coach shook my hand instead of his head.

The best part about being the biggest kid on the team? You don't go home from games discouraged anymore. You go home tired.

Sure enough, my carriage turned into a pumpkin once that season ended. That's because I grew a couple of inches the following summer and, wouldn't you know it, found myself back riding the bench the following year.

But I'd had my fifteen minutes of fame, except that it lasted for three months. An experience most kids can only dream about.

MY WISDOM:

"Tis better to have been a star for a moment than

never to have been a star at all."

Summer Camp at Oh-Goose-Me

"With boys you always know where you stand. Right in the path of a hurricane," —ERMA BOMBECK

I KNOW EVERYTHING THERE IS TO know about summer camp, I was shuffled off to one like clockwork, year after dependable year. So were my kids. And the kids of my kids were too, as soon as they were old enough to hunt snipes and weave lanyards. After all, parents need a break too, which means they'll often give up their football tickets or a new washing machine before they'll forego sending their kid to summer camp.

In my early summer camp days, I did my stints at a YMCA camp outside of Des Moines. I loved that camp, even though its rifles didn't shoot straight, its canoes leaked, and its counselors were more interested in the counselors at the adjoining YWCA camp than they were in us. Our camp was run like the world ought to be run—we could do anything we wanted to do as long as no one got killed doing it.

Times changed about the time I reached seventh grade—maybe my dad got a raise at his job – because he and Mom shooed me off to a hoity-toity summer camp complete with horses, sailboats, and clean towels. The camp was on the shore of a pristine lake in faraway

Minnesota and had a Native American name that I can't remember, but it sounded something like Oh-Goose-Me.

As fate would have it, I wasn't the only middle-class kid at Camp Oh-Goose-Me when I arrived. There was another kid like me at that camp like me, and his name was Frank, and he was from Iowa too.

The very first day at Camp Oh-Goose-Me, Frank and I learned that a girl scout camp was located directly across the lake from our camp. So, what choice did we have but to borrow one of Oh-Goose-Me's canoes in the dead of a moonlit night and quietly paddle to the far side of the lake. Once there, what else could we do but untie the flimsy knots on the girl's tents and die laughing as they came tumbling out of their tents like bats out of a cave at the stroke of midnight? Boy, was that fun!

As it turned out, Oh-Goose-Me's counselors weren't like the ones from my YMCA camp, which meant they were devoid of humor and understanding. Which also meant that the next day Frank and I were treated to an unscheduled train ride back to Des Moines.

Of course, Mom was at the train station to greet me. Talk about being devoid of humor and understanding!

MY WISDOM:

"Your mom will always love you but there will be

times when she will not like you."

Why Not to Wear Nice Clothes to School

"Part of the happiness of life consists not in fighting battles, but in avoiding them."
—NORMAN VINCENT PEALE."

IT TAKES A PRETTY SHABBY PERFORMANCE to give fist-fighting a bad name, but Whale Belly Turnquist and I managed, double-handedly, to do exactly that on one warm September day after school.

The trouble began in Mr. Walden's eighth grade history class. Perhaps it was a wayward spitball that started it all, or maybe a smart-ass remark. Whale Belly and I were plenty adept at both.

We met in the hallway after class, zit to zit, Converse to Converse. "The flagpole after school," I growled, burying my finger in his ample stomach. Whale Belly didn't come by his nickname by accident.

"Make my day Schell," Whale Belly snarled back. He was on the cutting edge where smart-ass remarks were concerned.

The flagpole after school was Roosevelt Junior High School's version of Madison Square Garden. A circular hedge surrounded the flagpole, turning it into a makeshift boxing ring. Many a score had been settled in its late afternoon shadows.

Word traveled fast. Plans were altered, bus schedules changed, bets were made. There was no turning back.

My upcoming beating of Whale Belly was, however, only a minor inconvenience compared to a bigger problem. Mom. It wasn't until the last class of the day that the realization hit me: my birthday had been the day before and I was wearing the new sweater and slacks she had bought, not exactly your ideal fighting togs. The worst beating Whale Belly could inflict on me paled in comparison to what she might do. She'd murder me in cold blood if I messed up those birthday clothes, or at least ground me until the end of the school year.

Enter Plan B.

I decided I'd run home after school and change into my fighting togs. So what if I was a few minutes late for the opening bell, they could start without me.

And so I ran home, changed clothes, then waved goodbye to one very suspicious mother. Chugging back to the flagpole, I found that my bad luck had continued. The multitudes were there, ready for the action.

Whale Belly was there too, looking like he'd rather be at the Tasty Treat snarfing down a root beer float than at the flagpole, about to have his face rearranged.

But the two of us *were* there—and so were the screaming multitudes—so what choice did we have? Let the games begin.

Whereupon Whale Belly and I waded into our version of what we thought a fight should be. And then and there, in front of God, our classmates, and whoever else might choose to join in, we set the sport of fist fighting back a century or more in just a few minutes.

Punch Miller, our school's number one tough guy, was in the audience, he'd stopped by for the laughs. (His nickname was short for One-Punch Miller because that's all it ever took). Finally, fortunately for everyone, Punch stepped in and broke up our facsimile of a fight. Thankfully for Whale Belly and thankfully for me, but ruefully for the disappointed multitudes.

Maybe we should make a universal rule.

Before people settle scores, before they start wars, they must first run home and change clothes.

MY WISDOM:

"If you think your mom wouldn't approve, you're

probably right. So don't do it."

A Boy's Rite of Passage:
The First Beer

"Without question, the greatest invention in the history of mankind is beer. Oh, I grant you that the wheel was also a fine invention, but the wheel does not go nearly as well with pizza." —DAVE BARRY

GROWING UP IS A SERIES OF monumental events, some more monumental than others. In an average kid's life, those events include the first word uttered, the first step taken, the first day at school, the first bike ride (two-wheelers only), the first kiss, and, of course, that hallowed rite of passage, the first beer.

In true American fashion, a kid can't have that first beer at home, sitting around the table with mom and dad. No sir, we need to have it far out in the woods where no one can see us or hear us. On a camping trip perhaps, with tents, campfires, and our best buddies at our side.

And so exactly that happened on a hot, steamy Saturday afternoon in the summer of 1949. Mom drove me to a path that led to a secret camping site alongside the Racoon River. My pals were already there, waiting.

"Be careful, honey," Mom warned when she dropped me off. Isn't that what moms always say when they think their kid is up to something?

"I will, Mom," I replied, in time-honored, kid fashion. Shouldering my backpack and clutching my sleeping bag, I closed the door to Mom's Dodge and crossed the street. I looked back over my shoulder—her car hadn't moved. She waved goodbye but wasn't smiling. I recognized the what's-he-up-to-now look clouding her face. I returned her wave and disappeared into the woods, heading for our secret camping site.

Who knew what adventures this night would bring? After all, it wasn't every day a kid was treated to a glimpse of his future and initiated into adulthood, both at the same time. And it wasn't every day that four eighth graders got their hands on two six-packs of beer.

The path to the camping site wound through a stand of elms, then emerged to cross the Santa Fe railroad tracks. A pheasant exploded from its hiding place, its frenzied flapping breaking the hush of the late afternoon. I paused, catching my breath as the Raccoon River below me cruised placidly by, on its way to meet with the Des Moines River. With renewed energy I tunneled through the thistles and brambles that shielded our sandbar campsite.

Emerging from the bushes, I spotted Bird and yelled "Got the beer?" Aha, the moment of truth.

Bird looked up from pounding tent stakes. "Bein' chilled," he grinned, pointing in the direction of the river.

A crackling campfire preceded dinner and I coated my stomach with a charred hamburger accompanied by a generous portion of hash browns smothered in burnt onions. A Coke to wash it all down and a Snickers candy bar concluded the feast.

"It's time," TK announced, his eyes wide behind owl-like glasses. "The beer should be cold."

Bird retrieved the two six-packs and I opened the inaugural beer of my life, using the can opener on my Boy Scout knife. (A tenth-birthday gift from Mom; if only she knew). "Pssst," the can sang, and I accepted my first mouthful of sin.

Well, warm prune juice would have been an improvement over the tepid, frothy liquid that tumbled down my throat and mixed with the curdling Snickers bar in my stomach.

"Wow," I choked. "Great stuff, this beer!"

"Putting it on my Wheaties in the morning," Dunk chimed in.

"Nectar of the Gods," cooed TK.

"Gotta pee," I announced a short time later, disappearing into the darkness. I emptied my bladder, along with the can of Budweiser, into the Raccoon River.

And that's how the rest of the evening went, for me anyway. Never "peed" so much in my life.

Finally, with the campfire a faint glow, Dunk and I lay in our sleeping bags and listened to the serenade of Iowa's mosquito squadrons.

"What a blast," Dunk said.

"Was it ever," I agreed. "Boy am I gonna pay in the morning though." Holding my head in feigned agony, I swore off Snickers bars forever.

"Me too," he replied, swatting a mosquito, then flicking the remains on my sleeping bag.

"Can't wait to do it again," I added.

"Yeah," Dunk yawned, his voice fading. "That beer sure goes right through you though, doesn't it? Must've peed a million times."

"Me too," I said, closing my eyes. "Next time we're gonna need more beer, though. Two six packs aren't enough."

MY WISDOM:

"It isn't about the first beer. It's about who you

were with when you had it."

When a Nickname Gets You in Trouble

"Nicknames stick to people, and the most ridiculous are the most adhesive."
—THOMAS CHANDLER HALIBURTON

THERE I SAT, COWERING IN THE office of Mr. Emmet J. Hasty, the principal of Roosevelt High School. And there Old Man Hasty sat, elbows folded, eyebrows arched, and lips pursed. Hasty had the look of a man with a need to use the bathroom, which didn't bode well for me. He was the undisputed emperor of Roosevelt High School and I wasn't the first kid to shake and quake in his office.

A drop of perspiration trickled down my cheek and splashed on Hasty's shiny linoleum floor. I wasn't handling this well and I'm sure Hasty was enjoying the experience.

A real live policeman stood beside the American flag that was on a stand in the corner of Hasty's office. Steely eyed, erect, and glaring, the cop was decked out with all the tools of his trade – badge, handcuffs, nightstick, accompanied by a grumpy scowl. Remember, this was the Fifties, when cops scared the hell out of kids. Today it's probably the other way around.

"Where were you last night, son?" Hasty growled, his jowls quivering. The silver clips on his suspenders glinted threateningly at me.

My frozen mind thrashed. Let's see . . . where was I last night? Who was I with? What did we do? My mind snapped shut like a steel gate and I slumped further down in the wooden chair. "I dunno, sir," I stammered, scratching my head. I wasn't kidding, I couldn't remember.

"Are you the kid they call Weasel?" the cop barked. If he'd been the smallest and skinniest kid on the eighth-grade basketball team, they'd call him Weasel too.

I nodded, eyes downcast and glued to the floor. I hated that nickname, which is probably why it stuck.

Hasty leaned forward; a cat hunkering down over a chipmunk. "Son, someone stole the March of Dimes container from the Tasty Treat Drive-in last night. The owner can remember the name of one of the kids in his establishment at the time the container disappeared. That name was Weasel."

Suddenly my mind came to life. That's it! That was where I was last night. The Tasty Treat. "The Tasty Treat, sir, that's where I was last night," I blurted triumphantly.

Too late. Guilty by perception.

Well, guilty in Hasty's perception anyway. In truth, the only thing I was guilty of was having a nickname I didn't like and a memory that went south when I was in trouble.

In the end, Hasty and the cop couldn't pin anything on me, and I walked out of the office a free kid. Chalk up a shallow victory for justice, but I was tarnished for life, in Hasty's mind anyway. It had to be that nickname.

I suppose I shouldn't care what Hasty thought; he'd be at least 130 today if he were still around. But I did care at that time, and so did my mom. Whooee, did she ever. No one was going to accuse her son of stealing without discussing it with her first.

Hasty didn't know how lucky he was when my Dad put his largely unused foot down and told Mom to settle down. "Let bygones be bygones," he instructed her firmly, and much to my relief, she took his advice and left the matter alone.

But personally, she couldn't let those bygones be bygones, so Hasty joined Dunk on her shit list. Where both would remain for as long as I can remember.

MY WISDOM:

"Never tell a kid he screwed up without telling his mom first. Then stand aside and let her do the telling."

The First Date: When Things Don't Go as Planned

"Forget the mistake. Remember the lesson."
—**Anonymous**

IT'S AN INDIAN SUMMER SATURDAY, EARLY October 1952. My driver's test successfully concluded the previous week, and my first real date utilizing Mom's aging Dodge was on the agenda. Wendy would be my date, we'd been to a couple of neighborhood movies before, thanks to Dad's shuttle service.

I'd been planning this occasion for months. My game plan was for an early movie, a quick visit to the Tasty Treat, followed by a late-night stop at somewhere secluded.

I scoped out several potential secluded sites that afternoon, finally settling on a cemetery across the street from a nearby shopping center. Close to home, it offered everything a first date-with-car required: quiet seclusion, free parking, and an unencumbered moon view.

Wendy had an eleven o'clock curfew, ditto for me. The early movie (From Here to Eternity) set the stage and the night was off to a fine beginning.

With the quick visit to the Tasty Treat concluded, Mom's past-its-prime Dodge chugged through the cemetery gate, past silent tombstones and canopied oak trees and into the depths of the cemetery. We arrived at my pre-selected location, the Dodge coughed, wheezed and then lurched to a stop.

The night was coal black, with the moon snoozing comfortably beneath a blanket of clouds. It was deathly quiet too, if you'll excuse the expression. Rows of tombstones loomed like silent sentinels and I realized my secluded spot didn't look as inviting at night as it did under the afternoon sun. I was worried, Wendy was frightened, and the scent of romance quickly faded, then disappeared. I locked the doors, cracked a window and we droned on nervously about school and friends. First base was on neither of our minds.

Finally, talked out and kissless, I glanced at my watch. It was only ten o'clock, but I twisted the key anyway and the Dodge awakened. We'd be home early—not exactly the end to the evening I'd envisioned.

"Ca-lump, ca-lump, ca-lump" came a strange noise from the rear of the Dodge as the car began to move. I stopped, grabbed the flashlight out of the glove compartment and got out of the car. Sure enough, the left rear tire was flatter than Butch Graff's crewcut.

Realizing I needed to change the tire, my mind began to thrash. I know people who were born to work with their hands. All they have to do is pick up a drill, a saw, or pliers, and somehow the drill drills, the saw saws and the pliers ply. Hand them a screwdriver and it screws; a wrench and it wrenches. The kind of people who can build things, fix stuff and complete chores ruin it for the rest of us.

I am not one of those people. Born a klutz, I am destined to die one. Even at the ripe young age of sixteen, I knew my fate; my klutziness was a lifetime sentence.

But . . . Wendy was watching and dabbing at her eyes. The whole school would know if I couldn't change that stupid tire.

I opened the trunk. I can honestly say I'd never looked inside the trunk of a car before. Oh, I'd pulled stuff out of trunks, like luggage and tools and baseball bats, and I'd stuffed things into trunks, like fishing equipment and tents and snow shovels, but I'd never really inspected a trunk. And I'd never, ever, peered underneath the bolted-down spare tire to see what all that tire-changing stuff was about or how it worked. It should have been part of the driver's test.

I dug deeper into the trunk and had no idea what that L-shaped dooleybob was supposed to do or how the thingamajig with the teeth worked. I studied those two foreign objects, carefully put them back where they belonged, and closed the trunk. Mom's Dodge would remain where it was until someone else came along to fix it.

I opened the door on Wendy's side of the car. She slid out and holding hands we walked out of the cemetery to the shopping center across the street. I called Dad on a pay phone and woke him up, which, I could tell, was not the highlight of his day. I could hear Mom in the background, grilling Dad with her what's-he-up-to-now questions.

Dad met Wendy and me at the phone booth then drove her home with me slumped in the back seat. Then we drove back to the waiting Dodge where I did my imitation of a highway maintenance worker standing idly by and watching him change the tire.

Finally, we made it home. Dad went to bed, while Mom made me a hot chocolate and went to work on my frazzled ego.

MY WISDOM:

"The first date is just for practice. You've gotta

start somewhere."

The View from Atop a Freight Train

"Work fills your pocket, but adventures fill your soul."
—ANONYMOUS

IT'S SUMMERTIME, CIRCA 1953—A STEAMY FRIDAY night when it felt like you had glue in your elbow creases and you couldn't bend your arm without it sticking. Our car filled with teenage rabble was aimlessly cruising the streets of Des Moines, as kids have been doing since automobiles replaced the horse.

"I'm bored," TK drawled out of nowhere. "I know what let's do. Let's hop a freight train."

"Sounds fun," I said without thinking, trying hard to sound as if TK had just suggested a chocolate sundae at the Tasty Treat. Anyway, come to think of it, it did sound kinda fun. Trains, to us landlocked kids, were what ocean freighters were to sea-dwelling folks. Powerful and purposeful, they spewed enchantment as they rumbled across our silent cornfields and headed for destinations unknown.

Our carful of teenage rabble deposited TK and me at the railroad switchyards and then squealed away, our friends laughing and shaking their heads. Rows of silent boxcars loomed silently in the darkness, brick-red elephants awaiting their master's command. We ducked and darted from boxcar to boxcar, in search of the perfect ride.

We finally selected a looming Santa Fe boxcar, its doors ajar, its destination westerly. Hand over hand we climbed to the top of the boxcar, wincing at every sound. Arriving at our topside destination, we leaned over the edge, balancing on one elbow, spying on the shadows below. We waited and waited, and the lure of adventure ebbed as the streets of Des Moines emptied and the world stood still.

Suddenly, without warning, the train jerked and shuddered, then rattled noisily forward, ever so slightly at first, gradually picking up speed. Faster and faster, and soon a cool evening breeze was splashing our faces. We were riding the rails, heading west, on our way to Omaha, Denver or even LA. The world was our destination as our adrenaline surged and overflowed.

The Santa Fe gathered speed and soon it was just TK and me and the groaning train. The staccato of the rails mesmerized us; visions of Marco Polo danced in our heads.

It wasn't long before the moon disappeared and the darkness turned inky black, and we shivered in our shirtsleeves. Still the Santa Fe pounded on, while any chance of punching in for my Saturday morning job waned and disappeared.

In case you're wondering, you don't just jump off a freight train whenever you feel like it, unless you've got a death wish. Those babies chug along at fifty miles an hour or better, and when you jump, there's no telling where you'll come to rest.

Finally, the beat of the rails slowed. Blinking specks of light welcomed us as we approached a small town, so we climbed partway down the side ladder. Then, clutching the ladder until the train showed signs of gathering speed again, we tucked our hearts in our throats and jumped into the early-morning emptiness and landed in the tall grass aside the railroad tracks.

TK and I walked into town, found a road heading east, and, for the next six hours, hitchhiked back to Des Moines. Mom greeted me at door when I finally made it home, first with an extra-long hug and then by grounding me for the remainder of the summer.

The punishment was worth the experience. Dad thought so too I could tell, although he knew better than to say so in front of Mom.

MY WISDOM:

"You'll regret more what you didn't do than what

you did do."

Just Because You Leave Home Doesn't Mean You'll Grow Up

"To those of you who received honors, awards and distinctions, I say well done. And to you C students, I say, you too may one day be president of the United States." —GEORGE W. BUSH

"But Mom . . ." I pleaded.

"There'll be no buts about it, James," she said, her hands on her hips. My red light flashed on—her use of the "James" word meant my fate was sealed. This conversation was only a preamble.

"Next year you'll be going to Drake for your sophomore year," she continued, then added for emphasis, "and you'll be living at home."

"But . . . but . . . I'll study harder next year, I promise," I pleaded, lamely. "I'll settle down. I really will, Mom, I was just . . ."

" . . . you were just disappointing your father and I," she replied, finishing my sentence for me, one of her favorite go-to tools when she was mad. "It's time you grow up and it's obvious Boulder isn't the best place for you to do that." Then she spun on her heels and headed for the kitchen, before turning around and facing me for her closing statement. The look on her face said this conversation was about to end.

"You'll live by our rules until you grow up. And you WILL grow up," she said, her brown eyes boring into mine. "Now go mow the lawn."

And with that, my life, as I'd known it during my freshman year in college, had come to an end.

What led to this conversation was me being a schmuck during my freshman year at the University of Colorado in Boulder. I'd spent my entire freshman year doing things that had nothing to do with education and everything to do with recreation. What I'd done would make no mother proud. Especially mine.

In my defense, it was easy to be a schmuck in Boulder back then. Boulder County had this incredible law that stated that 18-year-olds, immature or otherwise, could legally drink beer. (In Iowa, the magic number was 21). Boy, did I love that law; unbeknownst to Mom it was part of the reason I chose to go to CU in the first place.

Thanks to a focused commitment on my part, beer was now my number one favorite liquid on earth; early on in my freshman year I'd acquired a taste for Coors, Colorado's home-state beer. It didn't help that I lived in an apartment across the street from The Sink, Boulder's iconic watering hole. (Today, 60 years later it's still there, providing CU's students a place to unwind). It also didn't help that Coors was brewed just down the road in Golden, Colorado, and you could buy a dozen cases there and take them back to Iowa and sell them to your friends. For more than you paid for them, of course.

But beer was just the symptom. The overriding problem was that, in 1954, when I appeared on CU's campus, it was ranked #2 in Esquire Magazine's annual ranking of party schools. By the time I graduated in 1958, it was #1. Thanks to Mom and a year of living at home and forced growing up, I cleaned up my act and returned to Boulder for my junior year, a changed man. Thus, I didn't play an active role in CU achieving its lofty party school status. But I would have, had Mom not done what she was best at doing, which was making me grow up.

"A 1.56?" she'd gasped when she opened the letter that included my freshman-year grades. "Jim . . . how . . . how could you . . . ?", she'd stammered. Then her eyes turned glassy and she bowed her head.

That 1.56 cooked my goose, but it also saved my life. A sophomore year at Boulder would have killed me.

MY WISDOM:

"Love and support aren't always the answer.

Sometimes the cure must be penance."

PART TWO

GROWN UP. 1959-1996

While my three sons were growing up, I was growing up alongside them, both in terms of my work life and my personal life. I learned how to be a caring parent and they learned how to be rightminded adults. At age 33, following ten years of unsatisfying work, I stumbled upon entrepreneurship, a career I came to love. I'd made a lifetime marriage commitment before my senior year in college and twenty-six years later, at age 47, I broke that commitment. Trial and error would turn out to be my only teacher in this parenting and building-a-business phase of life, Dad died too early and Mom stayed busy in Phoenix, her new home.

Family spaghetti fest

Author at work

Mary & I

How to Have Fun Without Paying for It

"Life is like a train station, no matter how old the station might be, it still means something to someone."
—UNKNOWN

FOLLOWING THE BIRTH OF MY FIRST two children and a three-year stint in the Air Force, in 1963 our family of four moved to Moline, Illinois, a working-class town on the east side of the Mississippi River, across from my home state of Iowa. Moline wasn't Orlando or Anaheim when it came to things to do, but it had an inordinate number of fun and caring people and we soon numbered many of them as friends.

Well, maybe Moline didn't have a Disney World or Disney Land, but it did have trains that roared through town without stopping, both the big black ones that go *chug* and the sleek silver ones that go *whoosh*. Many of those trains originated in Chicago and, right on schedule, they'd chug or whoosh through Moline on their way to Denver or LA, day after interminable day.

All trains are exotic, to munchkins anyway, but it was the shiny silver ones that offered the finest entertainment a Sunday afternoon could buy. My friend Joe Murphy and I knew how to package the spectacle.

Joe had four munchkins and I had two (my third, Mike, was two years away) none of them taller than your belt buckle. We'd cram the six of them into Joe's station wagon on a Sunday afternoon and, following a stop at Whitey's Ice Cream for a chocolate phosphate or strawberry malt, we'd make a beeline for Moline's 6th Avenue train station.

The 6th Avenue station had been abandoned for years, all its windows were broken, and the few remaining shards of glass had grayed with the stains of time. The chipped and cracked concrete passenger platform, a veteran of countless hugs and tears, sagged wearily, a deserted temple grown old without grace.

As soon as we arrived, the station wagon would empty and each of our munchkins would place a penny on the rail, soon to be added to their expanding collection of flattened one cent pieces. A few minutes before four o'clock, right on schedule, one of them would kneel, and with an ear to the rail shout the exciting news.

"Here comes the Zephyr," would come the shrill cry.

And then, before you could hum the first bar of the Star-Spangled Banner, the Zephyr would thunder upon us, a silver bullet piercing the shadows of the late afternoon. The ground would shake and our teeth would rattle. And then, as quickly as it came, the Zephyr would be gone, and the sound of silence would reign supreme.

Oh, one more thing I almost forgot: The best part of the spectacle. The whistle.

Just for a minute, close your eyes and pretend you were the engineer piloting that thundering Zephyr. What would you do as your train approached a troupe of dancing, screaming, waving, munchkins, jumping up and down on the platform of a tired and abandoned train station?

Come on now, admit it . . . you'd give your whistle a hearty blast. And maybe even a double one if you were having a good day.

Well, the Zephyr's engineers usually were having a good day, which meant that, more often than not, the whistle would blow twice. And when it did it would make our munchkins' day. And sometimes their week.

And it kinda made their life too, if you know what I mean.

MY WISDOM:

"Who needs Disneyland or Vegas, the best entertainment can often be found right at home."

A Recommendation for Doctor Seuss

"You can find magic wherever you look. Just sit back and relax, all you need is a book." —DR. SEUSS

DOCTOR SEUSS WAS TO MY KIDS what the Dalai Lama was to his followers; the master of the universe with all the right answers. As a result, Seuss and his books were as much a part of my three sons' upbringing and survival as their friends, their teachers, and the hospital emergency room.

Does the following scenario sound familiar?

You walk in the door following another stressful day at work. "Whew, I can't wait for my beer," you're thinking, as you stumble in the door. You'll only have one, before dinner, just to drive the taste of the day away.

"Hi honey," your wife replies, breathing a sigh of relief. "Before you have your beer, will you please read Doctor Seuss to Mike. He's been waiting all day."

And so, you postpone your hallowed beer and out comes the frayed pages of Doctor Seuss. And nobody, not Mike, not Mom, not even the good Doctor himself, knows the lines of *Cat in the Hat* any better than you do. That's because Doctor Seuss hasn't read the book as many times as you have and neither has Mom, while Mike can't read at all. But what Mike can do is to stare at every picture and point out every detail and fuss over every word, while you're having visions of how good that beer is going to taste.

I know what I'm talking about when it comes to Doctor Seuss, incidentally—I've read his books more times than I've tied my shoes. But I wish he'd have added another element to the scope of his writing, I wish he'd have written a book for us. The people doing the reading. The parents. The moms and the dads. You and me.

Sure, Seuss did a commendable job of explaining to our kids the difference between good and bad, happy and sad, right and wrong. But we parents need to be educated too in order to follow up on those lessons that our kids are learning from the good doctor.

Looking back, I know now that we needed Seuss's help even more than our kids. After all, our kids had us to lead them and show them the way, but who did we have? Our own parents, perhaps, if they happened to live nearby or would be close to the phone when we'd call. But even then, thanks to the decades that had passed since they had raised us, our parents didn't always have the right answers. We're walking proof of that.

If you were like me, your parents lived time zones away. And many of them, similar to my mom and dad, had moved on to the next stage of their life. They'd had their fill of parenting; once around that long block was enough. Besides, parenting changes over time, in sync with the rest of the world. It's not surprising that grandparents are somewhere out in left field, at least where the day-to-day stuff is concerned. It was that way when I was raising my kids and it was that way when my kids were raising their kids. Grandparents had their limitations.

If only the good doctor had tried to help us parents at the same time he was helping our kids. While he played a role in shaping their lives for those thirty minutes when we came home from work or before we put them to bed, it was us who were doing the shaping the rest of the time.

The rest of the time. When Seuss's books were resting quietly on the shelves, waiting for Dad to come home.

MY WISDOM:

"It's a tossup between who needs the direction of

Dr. Seuss the most: we parents or our kids."

My Son Teaches Me Yet Another Lesson in Life

"It's alright to cry. But for the right reasons".
—ANONYMOUS

ELEVEN-YEAR-OLDS ARE THE WORST. BY "THE worst," I mean they're the hardest to control. Maybe control is the wrong word, because nobody really "controls" an eleven-year old. "Shape" might be a better word.

And someone with rock-solid credentials had better be around to do the shaping. And whoever that someone is had better have his feet planted firmly on the ground. Firmly on the ground, like a rock on a mountain or a sequoia in a forest. That person had better be someone . . . well . . . someone like me. A hardened and grizzled veteran, a frazzled survivor, and a dad toughened by the lessons of life.

To illustrate . . .

My son Mike was eleven when he and I attended the movie *ET* together. It was a Saturday in the early fall, the theater was packed with legions of other dads, many of whom, like me, would rather be mowing the lawn, watching football, or taking an afternoon nap.

But there we all were, ready to watch a movie so ridiculous it defied adult logic.

Extra-terrestrial? Now reeeeeally. What kind of a nincompoop would buy such a premise, I thought at the time? Who in their right mind would spend their hard-earned money to watch a sawed-off wart from a far-away planet try to capture the heart of a kid? What kind of a numbskull could get wrapped up in such a tale?

Me, that's what kind of a numbskull.

And the further the movie progressed, the more wrapped up I became. Until finally, when ET's heart light flickered and went out, one tear spiraled down my cheek and then another. Then the dam burst, and I turned away, hoping Mike wouldn't catch his hardened and grizzled dad, bawling like a lost heifer. Over a movie, no less.

Alas, my evasiveness didn't work, Mike caught me, dead to rights. I must have splashed him.

When the movie was finished and the two of us walked outside, the late afternoon sun illuminated my splotched face. Mike put his arm around my waist.

"Shake it off, Dad," he said, wiping his own eyes on his sleeve. "Crying isn't just for kids, you know.

"It's OK for dads to cry too."

MY WISDOM:

"Sometimes it feels good to be a kid again, even if

it's only when watching a movie."

The Truth about Kid's Sports

*"Do you know what my favorite part of the game is?
The opportunity to play."* —MIKE SINGLETARY

LIKE EVERYTHING ELSE IN TODAY'S WORLD, kids' sports have
changed. The games that kids play are no longer played by kids'
rules, in someone's back yard, with a ragtag collection of neighborhood friends as teammates or competitors. Rather, most of today's
kid games are played by adult rules, in real-life ball parks, arenas,
and stadiums, with teams of 12-year-olds dressed up in uniforms
that, when I was a kid, we only saw in pictures of our favorite major
leaguers.

Too many of kid's sports today are organized and scheduled
events, oftentimes with paying fans in the stands, eating peanuts
and popcorn and waving pom-poms. Those orchestrated games are
intended, no doubt, to educate and enlighten our emerging adults,
preparing them to become upstanding citizens.

The problem with this scenario is that our kids aren't sure about
what they're expected to learn from the game they're playing,
besides chucking a baseball at warp speeds or shooting a basketball like LeBron James. That's because they don't understand the
rules we adults have established in order to teach them the lessons
they're not old enough to grasp.

For instance, in 1973 I was the coach of my son Mike's hockey team. Mike was a Mite; the littlest of the little, ages seven and eight. In addition to Mites, there were also the Squirts, Pee Wees, Bantams and Midgets. Hockey people think small.

Ninety-nine percent of all Mite hockey players skated like drunken sailors. The other one percent skated like the hockey equivalent of Michael Jordan, the result of which is that, in every Mite game, we observers were treated to an ebbing and flowing pack of drunken sailors chasing one sober Michael Jordan.

So, what happens next?

Why, Michael Jordan goes nuts and scores a multitude of goals, that's what happens next, which means his team always wins and everyone thinks the coach is a reincarnated Vince Lombardi. This situation has not gone unnoticed by youth hockey's ruling bodies however, which accounts for a myriad of complicated rules that, in the interest of fairness, are designed to minimize Michael Jordan's time on the ice, thereby allowing more playing time for the drunken sailors. Not surprisingly, those rules are often offset by the creativity of Michael's coaches, creativity designed to maximize Jordan's time on the ice and win the game for the home team.

I had a Michael Jordan on my Mite team—it wasn't my Mike, he was a drunken sailor. It was crunch time—the playoffs—which meant if we lost, we'd hang up our skates and the season would be over. The problem was, the other team had a Michael Jordan on their team too, and they were ahead by one goal with less than two minutes to play.

My Michael had used up all his allotted ice time and was perched unhappily on our team's bench. As the clock ticked down, a stream of concerned parents sidled up to the snowdrift I was standing in – the game was being played outdoors. "Get Jordan's butt back on the ice," several of them let me know, in one version or another. Hockey parents aren't subtle when crunch time comes around.

But I didn't get Jordan's butt back on the ice and we ended up losing the game by one goal. Our season ground to a halt.

Following the game-ending whistle, my Mike and I trudged back to the warming house and began the age-old, skate-lace-untying-with-frozen-fingers routine. Hushed whispers abounded from the gaggle of my team's parents; it was obvious I was not being considered for coach-of-the-year honors. Quickly, Mike and I walked to the car, the glazed, frozen snow squeaking underfoot. Mike was broodingly quiet.

We arrived at the car and his silence continued. I opened the door, tossed his stick and skates in the back seat, while he slid into the passenger seat, his helmet askew. Silently he stared at the dashboard.

I slipped gingerly behind the wheel, well, as gingerly as one could while wearing fifty pounds of insulated clothing. As I glanced under Mike's helmet and stocking cap, his pensive look thickened.

Finally, he turned to me. Our eyes met.

"Dad," he said, "I've been wondering if . . . "

Oh, oh, I gulped, bracing myself. Here it comes.

" . . . I can sleep over at Richey Ragatz's house tonight?"

So, there you have it. See what I mean about kids not understanding why adults play their games? Can you imagine Michael Jordan wanting to sleep over at Magic Johnson's house after losing a season-ending playoff game?

Maybe it isn't our kids that don't understand the way games should be played and the reason we play sports in the first place.

Maybe, just maybe, it's us.

MY WISDOM:

"99% of the kids who play youth sports are not going to get a college scholarship. Chances are your kid will be one of them. Let 'em have fun."

A Surefire Way to Quit Smoking

"For more information on lung cancer, keep smoking."
—THE LUNG ASSOCIATION OF BRITISH
COLUMBIA

IT'S 1968, I'M IN MY EARLY thirties, a bit overweight, a tad out of shape, and not quite ready for the Iron Man Triathlon. To make matters worse, I also smoked cigarettes. No, make that I mainlined nicotine, in the form of unfiltered Camels, the dumbest choice a smoker could ever make. I reduced a pack a day to ashes, sometimes more, especially when I was bored.

Furthermore, being of humble pedestrian stock, I inhaled.

During a crisp Minneapolis Friday in October 1968, I returned to my office from a late afternoon business appointment. I parked my aging Mercury in the office parking lot and, since I'd be heading home in less than an hour, and since my time was so incredibly valuable I couldn't waste one nanosecond of it, I left the keys in the ignition. I wouldn't be but a minute.

Bad move on my part. Three high school kids on their way home from school spotted my Merc. And the keys. Along with the opportunity.

"Hey, Jim," shouted Paul, one of my co-workers across the hall with a view of the parking lot. "Isn't that your Merc disappearing over the hill?"

I sprinted to the window in his office and peered out. Sure enough, there was an empty space in the parking lot where my car used to be.

Paul and I piled in his car and headed in the same direction the Merc and its carful of teenage bandits had been going before it disappeared. Through winding suburban streets, around corners and past stop signs we sped. Fifteen minutes went by and there was still no sign of my purloined Merc—we'd come up empty handed. Except that, on the way back to the office, we rounded a corner and there my car sat, resting placidly alongside the curb in a tree-lined, suburban neighborhood. The three young thieves were just emerging; the driver was locking the door. It was a Friday evening, they were heading home for dinner, but would be back to pick up the car.

Paul's car screeched to a halt, the two of us jumped out and I made a beeline for the driver. The kid threw the car keys at me, but it would take more than a handful of car keys to slow me down. By God, that kid had stolen my car and he wasn't going to get away with it. And then it was the old Keystone Kops routine, suburban neighborhood style. I wanted that kid, so I lumbered after him as he sprinted away. Through front yards and backyards, over fences and under clotheslines, the chase raged on.

Remember, I was lugging around more than a few pounds I didn't need, plus I was dissipated and slow, yet there I was, chasing a kid who was lithe, young and fast. But I had one huge advantage over him—something of mine that was running a lot faster than his.

My adrenaline!

I mean, I was crazed. That was my *car* the kid had heisted, it belonged to me. Sure, it was no Corvette, but it got me where I was going and besides, it was paid for.

After ten minutes of suburban steeplechase, me and my adrenaline overtook the kid and his youth. Panting for breath, he collapsed beneath a backyard clothesline, looking up at me from underneath a row of underwear and towels.

Vindicated, I dragged the kid off to a rendezvous with the cops, and then the trusty Merc and I chugged our way home. I was exhausted, but the Merc was still mine.

Once home, I walked into the house and promptly began throwing up. This went on for three days and three nights and I couldn't keep anything down: soup, 7 Up, or water. Even oxygen was tough. It was agony to breathe, but what was the option, so I wheezed and coughed and spit up green crud. It was agony to open my eyes, but it was hell to close them.

Smoke a cigarette? Surely you jest.

It was scary what was going on inside of that body of mine; something had revolted where all my working parts toiled. My insides were enraged, and they weren't the least bit shy about letting me know. "If you ever smoke so much as one more cigarette again," my working parts screamed, "you can find a new body to haul you around."

So, what else could I do but quit smoking?

Looking back, I owe the kid who stole my car a favor. Thanks to him, it's fifty years later and I'm still here to tell this story.

MY WISDOM:

"Why does it take a crisis to kill a bad habit?"

Little Things Mean a Lot

"You can't live a perfect day without doing something for someone who will never be able to repay you."
—JOHN WOODEN

TIM WAS TWELVE YEARS OLD WHEN we first met. Bordering on skinny with a thatch of unruly black hair, he owned a smile as wide as the Mississippi River. Tim was an overachiever if ever there were one, and I'll bet he's still that way today.

How can you not love over-achievers? The kind of people who play the game, work the job, or live the life, a notch above where their abilities lie? Ask them for two, they give you three. Send them for silver, they bring home gold. They aim low, they achieve high, and everyone wins.

Tim. Over-achiever extraordinaire. Learner and listener exceptionale, he was the center iceman on my Pee Wee hockey team.

It was late in October, one month into the hockey season, when I first heard the news. Tim's dad, a good man, supportive father, and ardent hockey fan, had been diagnosed with cancer and was given two months to live.

Quickly bedridden, his father would never see Tim skate again. Yet the boy never missed a practice or a game and skated every shift as if he were late for Thanksgiving dinner. He listened hard and played hard, all the time overachieving in his quiet, resolute way. The smile was still there, although not quite as wide as it used to be.

Two weeks before Christmas, I wrote Tim's father a letter, a dad-to-dad kind of note. I told him what it was like to borrow his son for a few hours every week. I gave him a glimpse of Tim through an outsider's eyes, a view he could never have on his own.

Two weeks later Tim's dad passed away. It was the day after Christmas.

Our team attended the funeral en masse—fourteen twelve-year olds in matching green jackets and me in a rumpled navy suit. Tim's head turned as we walked down the aisle of the church. He glanced at his teammates and then at me, and I caught a faint trace of that smile.

Thanks for being here, he seemed to say.

Tim returned to the team following the New Year holiday and played better and harder than before. The team jelled and so did Tim; his dad would have been proud.

One day in early February my phone rang.

"Jim, this is Tom, Tim's uncle. I'm calling to say thanks."

I mumbled something inane in return. I knew what was coming, I don't handle such messages well.

"You'll never know what your letter meant to my brother," Tom went on. "He read it every day. It was on his bedside table when he died."

"Thanks, Tom," I mumbled, goosebumps rising. "I'm sorry I couldn't do more."

It was only a letter. One sheet of paper with a few well-chosen words. Took fifteen minutes to write.

But what a difference it had made in Tim's Dad's remaining time.

And, as it turned out, in mine.

MY WISDOM:

"The biggest gifts come wrapped in the smallest

packages."

It's OK to Fail, Just Don't Waste It

"My son is now an entrepreneur. That's what you're called when you don't have a job." —TED TURNER

IT'S 1968 AND MY VAPID BUSINESS career was snoozing along, going nowhere fast. I was working for a timber/lumber company in St. Louis Park, Minnesota, we manufactured and sold a mish-mosh of wood products, most of which were treated with nasty wood-preservative chemicals like creosote and pentachlorophenol and other snarky stuff. Our products included such scintillating offerings as telephone poles, barn poles, and fence posts.

At the same time, two of my three sons were involved in Minnesota's favorite winter pastime . . . youth hockey. The youngest hockey players, which included my kids, had to hone their skills on outdoor ice, since our community's indoor ice was being used by the older kids. The problem with that? Even in frigid Minnesota the winter sun can take its toll on outdoor ice; the outside temperature can be well below freezing but if the sun is out, its rays will melt the ice.

My idea to resolve this dilemma?

Keep the sun off the ice with a roof. Duh. That roof would be an inexpensive roof supported by a cobweb-looking maze of . . . you guessed it . . . fence posts; fence posts from my company, of course.

That was the idea anyway, which, if it worked, would help my employer sell his fence posts and give my kids a longer hockey season.

I took this idea to the Park and Rec Department of a nearby Minneapolis suburb, and, miracle of miracles, they bought it. The resulting roof-supporting structure was designed by a Minneapolis engineering firm and resembled, in scientific parlance, a geodesic dome. The good news is that the cobweb-like, geodesic-dome-looking maze of fence posts would support a roof even if it had four feet of wet snow on top of it.

Great idea, right? A roof built out of inexpensive fence posts. Geodesic dome. First ever using wood. In the world.

I could be the last ever, too. Putting the damn thing together was a nightmare. You think the Golden Gate Bridge was tough to assemble.

But the project was eventually completed, and that suburb's wee hockey tykes had a roof over their head for years to come. Everyone was happy.

Well, not quite. The project was sold for X but it cost XXX to assemble. My boss never told me how much XXX was. Whatever it was, he wasn't happy.

Thanks to that financial failure, I learned that I needed to work for someone else the rest of my life. That someone else was me. So, I borrowed money from my family and friends and bought a Minneapolis sporting goods business out of bankruptcy, officially kicking off my entrepreneurial career.

Steven Jobs, one of the world's consummate entrepreneurs, once said "here's to the crazy ones. The misfits, the rebels, the ones who see things differently."

Jobs didn't say here's to the crazy ones that can't hold down a regular job, but he could have. I was one of those, in part because I was, well, crazy, where business was concerned anyway. I knew nothing about construction and yet I sold a building with a roof made out of – I'm not making this up – wooden fence posts.

Wooden fence posts? Are you kidding me?

And then, shortly thereafter, I knew nothing about owning a business and yet I bought one that someone else had screwed up. Borrowed money from my family and friends to do it, too. Twenty years later, I knew little about writing and yet I started a writing career at age 55. Not to mention a publishing business twenty-five years after that. Which I didn't know anything about either.

My life has been sprinkled with crazy stuff, where my business career was concerned, anyway. Crazy stuff I knew little or nothing about. Screenprinting, for instance, or sporting goods, or racquetball clubs, all were businesses I started in the 60's. Starting those businesses sounded like a good idea at the time, so what could I do but dive in. Fortunately, all of them worked, and by 1990 I'd sold them all. (Sadly, none are around today, although the sporting goods business held on until 2019).

In addition to being one of the crazy ones, I was also one of the lucky ones. One of the lucky ones who had finally found a career I could love. Never mind that it took a failure to find it. (For more on this subject, see the chapter "Find a Career You Can Love" in Part Four of this book).

I was also lucky to get an early glimpse of my future career when I was a kid, thanks to Jack and our entrepreneurial venture into the used-golf-ball business. Which ultimately failed when Jack bit the postman. Bad dog.

Somewhere in everyone's background there's will be a failure with a message imbedded in it. The trick is to turn that message into something you can touch, feel, and enjoy.

Like a career, for instance.

MY WISDOM:

"It's OK to fail, but only if you act on the lesson

you learn from the failure."

When Work Collides with Family

"Time is the coin of your life. It is the only coin you have and only you can determine how it is spent. Be careful lest you let other people spend it for you."
—CARL SANDBERG

IT WAS A BRIGHT, WARM WEEKDAY in May, the kind of day that makes the drizzly days of spring worth the wait. Minneapolis's freeways were characteristically clogged as another workday wound down. It was a perfect day for Dad to come home after work, toss a frisbee with Todd, help Mike with his homework, and slip the dog a few scraps under the dinner table.

Sorry, but that wouldn't be happening on this day. Instead I found myself, tired and lonely at O'Hare Airport in Chicago, surrounded by throngs of unruly strangers. Hundreds of them, all tired and crabby, traveling from Point A to Point B and maybe even Point C.

"We're sorry, Mr. Schell," the Northwest Airlines ticket agent had shrugged. "The plane you'll be taking to Jacksonville has been held up in Detroit. We don't have a time of arrival yet."

So, what should I have done? Screamed at the agent? Pounded my fist? Feigned a seizure? I'd nixed those reactions – they never seem to help. Besides, the guy in front of me had tried them already.

I nodded mutely. The agent shrugged, then turned his tired eyes back to his computer screen.

I found a seat that offered a view of the masses passing by, some rushing, some straggling. A beer might help, but then I nixed the thought. I'd fall asleep and miss my Jacksonville flight.

What happened with my kids today, I wondered? Did Jim get his test scores back? Did Todd win his hockey game? Mom will have to read Dr. Seuss to Mike tonight.

I watched the harried travelers filing by: on and on they came, rarely a smile on their frozen faces. Tears of goodbye on the faces of a few, frowns of stress on others.

Small wonder with all the stress. Flights late or cancelled. Connections missed. Gates changed. Tickets misplaced. Luggage lost. Raincoats forgotten. Glasses left on the plane.

Been there, done 'em all.

And still the hordes plodded on. One gate emptied, another one filled. Business folks led the parade with their drab suits, bulging briefcases, and luggage hooked over slumped shoulders. Onward and onward they came, determined, purposeful, yet colorless, like the lemmings in Apple's iconic commercial.

Time crawled by. A vacationing family, complete with wailing baby and pouting kids, hunkered down nearby, digging into a greasy sack of airport food. Newlyweds wandered by, hands entwined, oblivious to the rest of us.

An attractive woman passed by, heels clicking on the tiled floor, avoiding the looks of traveling men. A basketball team here, a volleyball team there, a kid's soccer team with its entourage of catatonic adults.

I should be getting a jump on tomorrow's work instead of watching the people parade, I reminded myself. Reviewing a file for my morning meeting, rehearsing my pep talk for the location manager, sketching an outline for Jacksonville's turnaround.

Nuts to reviewing, rehearsing, and sketching, it can come later. I'll call home instead.

I should have reviewed, rehearsed, and sketched. Jim got his test scores back and they weren't what he'd hoped. Todd lost his hockey game.

I reminded myself that travel was a necessary part of the businessman's M.O. My employees need jobs, my vendors need customers, and my kids need to go to college someday.

And I need the adrenaline rush that comes from the work I do.

MY WISDOM:

"There's a price to be paid for everything we do.

The trick is balancing the cost against the benefit."

Fathers Are Like Small Dogs

"God created man, but I could do better."
—ERMA BOMBECK

WHETHER WE LIKE IT OR NOT, sooner or later our kids start exhibiting signs of becoming an adult. They're preparing, or so society tells us anyway, to make the transformation to the next phase of life – that phase where they change from being on the receiving end of parental advice to the giving end.

This reversing-of-roles phase is not to be taken lightly. Early adulthood, as we scarred veterans have learned, is no leisurely stroll with the wind at our back, but rather a tumultuous transition into the face of a hurricane. There's a long list of skills and traits our kids need in order to ensure a healthy adulthood, including a predisposition to logic, coolness under fire, and knowing how to protect the household against unwelcome invaders.

Who better to provide examples of such attributes than me— one of the most logical and coolest-under-fire fathers the world has ever known.

Or so I once thought.

Midnight had come and gone as I stared out the bedroom window watching the leaves of the maple tree in our front yard dance gently in October's soft breeze. I'd been rehearsing the next day's

meeting with my company's bankers as the night droned intermi-
nably on. It'd been a tough year.

Suddenly an angular shadow flitted past the window. I sat up in
bed, shaking the cobwebs away. Then another shadow, and another.
I slid from the bed to the floor, my heart rattling. Those shadows
had substance.

The shadows flitted again and again. There were two, maybe
three, midnight intruders, casting their shadows, invading our yard.

I needed help, I realized. Wide-eyed now with adrenaline pump-
ing, I tiptoed quietly down the stairs to the basement level of our
home and roused my oldest son Jim, sturdy high school senior,
hockey and football player. My hand over his mouth, I whispered
"shhh, follow me. Someone's outside."

We stole back upstairs in boxer shorts, hugging the staircase wall.
Reaching the front door, I peeked out the window. The shadows
were still there, bobbing, weaving.

"I'll hit the porch light and we go," I whispered, and Jim nodded
mutely. He was still half asleep.

One hand on the doorknob now, I flicked on the porch light and
threw open the door. Crashing after the nearest shadow, I shouted
for Jim to pursue another of the shadows and off he plunged into
the bushes bordering our neighbor's yard.

Pumped with adrenaline, I caught my prey just as we reached the
street in front of our house. A lunging tackle and I felt my knees and
elbows shred, followed by the dull thud of bodies connecting with
concrete. Silence returned to the neighborhood.

I stood, elbows and knees screaming. The fallen shadow was
sprawled, facedown, on the street, stirring, yet silent. Jim returned
from his chase, framed by the soft ribbons of the streetlight.

"I lost him, Dad," he gasped, breathing hard. He spotted the form
stretched out on the pavement. "What . . . what happened?"

Without answering I knelt to get a closer look at the midnight
intruder.

"My God, Dad," Jim gasped, as the intruder rolled over and
looked up at him. "It's a girl."

I stare incredulously at her soft face and frightened eyes, her forehead dabbed with blood.

"Dad, it's Laurie Hanson. She's a football cheerleader."

In unison we turned and faced the house. Streamers of toilet paper dangled from the maple tree, fluttering softly in the post-midnight breeze.

I'd tackled a cheerleader.

Gently, we helped her up, walked her inside the house, and pressed a cold washcloth against her forehead. Her two shaken friends reappeared and finally, thirty minutes later, following sheepish good-byes, the house was quiet again.

I met with Laurie's parents the following day and pled guilty to over-reacting. Graciously accepting my apology, they knew from past experience why fathers do what they do in the dark of the night.

They understood why fathers protect their household, whether or not it needs protecting.

MY WISDOM:

"Fathers are like small dogs, they growl, snap, and gnash their teeth when they think their space is being invaded."

When a Father Loses His Way

"Dad taught me everything I know. Unfortunately, he didn't teach me everything he knows." —AL UNSER

FATHERHOOD CAN BE A BITTERSWEET EXPERIENCE, sometimes more bitter than sweet, if the father lets the distractions of life get in his way. Which leads me to this story of one father I met who lost his way, soon to be followed by his son.

A young friend of mine, an employee in my business, endured a bout with alcohol. His family finally intervened, and he enrolled in a Minneapolis recovery program. In the course of the program he asked if I'd take part in it as a friend, employer, and, well, as a pseudo father, since his own father, thanks to eight other children at home, had his hands full with other problems at the time.

My role? A sponsor, the program called it. I'd take part in the confrontational process, hold my young friend's hand, and, as it turned out, be an unwitting observer of a scene I'd never forget.

In one phase of the meetings, the person being confronted is required to pull up a chair in the center of a circle that includes his peers and their invited sponsors. The person in the chair then braces himself for "feedback." The process goes something like this:

Round One: Sponsors or family members recite all the dirty rotten things their friend or relative has done while in the depths of dependence. No holds barred.

Round Two: Sponsors or family members relate why, despite all the person's misdeeds, he is still special to them. Why they're in this circle, anyway. Why they want their friend to be the person he is capable of being.

One of the class members, named Billy, was the son of Mr. Gotrocks, an over-achieving Minneapolis businessman. You know the type, too much time raising capital and not enough time raising kids. So, what do most kids of overachieving adults do in situations like that? Why, they raise holy hell just to piss the old man off—if they can't get his attention one way, they'll get it another.

Billy's time in the hot seat came up and I was sitting in the perimeter of the circle, observing, along with a dozen or so of Billy's peers and their sponsors. In Round One, right on cue, the dad unloaded on Billy as only an aggrieved father can. I mean, he emptied both barrels, and we onlookers squirmed as the evidence piled up. Guilty as charged, the facts proclaimed; an open and shut case. The father spared no details.

Then it was time for Round Two. The this-is-why-I-love-you-despite-all-the-crap-you've-pulled part of the program.

Well, Mr. Gotrock's mouth opened, but nothing came out.

Nothing came out because he had nothing to say. He didn't know his son well enough to say anything nice about him, I assumed, so he couldn't say anything at all.

So, what could Gotrocks do but examine his fingernails and adjust his tie and mumble something that only he understood. Then he and Billy began trading daggers again.

"Tell me, Mr. Gotrocks," the meeting's female facilitator asked softly. "Do you love your son?"

"Er, uh, well . . . yes" Billy's dad mumbled, wiping a speck of dust from his wingtip shoes.

"And when was the last time you told him you loved him?"

"Er, uh, well . . . " came the muttered reply again, followed by a shrug.

"Tell me," she continued, undeterred. "When was the last time you hugged your son?"

A hunch of the shoulders was the man's only reply.

Leaving Gotrocks to stew, she turned to Billy and asked him the same questions, followed by similar answers. You could hear a pin drop.

Looking the father in the eyes, she then asked, "would you like to tell your son you love him?"

He nodded his head ever so slightly.

"And would you like to hug him?"

Another slight nod.

Same questions to Billy. Similar responses.

"Please stand," she gently commanded the two of them. Father and son stood.

"Well," she said, smiling. "So, what are you waiting for? Get on with it."

Whereupon father and son stared into foreign eyes. Then their foreheads grew damp, their knees quivered, and the two men eyed each other like a fly would an approaching spider. Finally, they extended their arms and damned if they didn't get on with it, right there, in front of God and the facilitator and a room filled with people they didn't know.

And that hug turned into an embrace and then into a tear-filled clutch and from that a vice-like clamp. And there they remained for what seemed like an eternity, and the image will be stamped in my mind for the rest of my life.

"I love you, Billy," the father finally whispered.

"I love you too, Dad," the son sobbed.

And, I swear, the two of them would still be in that vicelike grip if the facilitator hadn't broken them up, sat them down, and talked to all of us about the responsibilities of fatherhood in making a family work.

The family comes first, she told us, if something isn't working on the homefront, it's up to the father to fix it. That's what fathers do, she said, they are put on this earth to make the problems that trouble their family go away.

"After all, that's what you're supposed to do when you're running your business, isn't it?" she said, her eyes fixed on Billy's dad.

"Why should a family be any different?"

MY WISDOM:

"When a family isn't working, the buck stops

with Dad."

When a Lawyer Calls with Good News

"Lawyers are the only profession I know where the more there are, the more there are needed."
—ROBERT LUCKY

NOTHING GOOD, NOTHING THAT I CAN remember anyway, ever came as a result of a phone call from an unknown lawyer. Until, that is, one sundrenched, San Diego day in the summer of '91.

My son Mike was visiting us on his way to Thailand, for reasons vague to us all. His vagabond blood runs deep.

Mike left our house in the morning for an all-day, ocean skirting bike ride from Carlsbad to La Jolla and back again. At day's end, he was pedaling east, framed by a fiery, late-afternoon sun, when an oncoming car, its driver temporarily blinded by the sun, swerved into his lane, sending Mike and bike flying.

When the dust had settled, Mike's only injury was a hairline gash. A two-hour wait in the emergency room and ten stitches later, Mike was home for six o'clock dinner, his appetite intact.

The next morning the telephone rang. A man's voice asked for Mike.

"Mike, my name is Dennis. I'm an attorney for the Acme Insurance Company. We're sorry about yesterday's accident with one of our policyholders. How are you feeling today?"

"Aw, I'm OK. Ten stitches was all. No big deal."

"Is there anything we can do for you?"

"Well, I'm leaving for Thailand in two weeks. I'd like to make sure the hospital bill is paid before I leave."

"No problem," the voice on the phone cooed. "Send the bill to my attention. I'll see that it's paid the same day it arrives. Is there anything else?"

"Nah, the bike's okay. Just pay the hospital."

"How would you like a check for $1,500?"

"How . . . how . . . would I like a *what* for what?"

"A check. For $1,500. After you sign a waiver of course."

"What's the check for?"

"Your trip to Thailand. We want to help you enjoy yourself on the trip and we're sorry for any inconvenience our driver may have caused."

Which is how, in exchange for ten stitches and a signed waiver, Mike became $1,500 richer. A trade he would gladly had made if he were offered the opportunity again.

Now why didn't I, veteran of this paranoid world, anticipate Mike's conversation with that insurance company? Why didn't I give him a heads up that this conversation was coming? What have I been doing all my life? Working crossword puzzles?

I mean, what are dads for, anyway? I could have at least advised him on how to negotiate with the lawyer. Chances are, $2,500 was what the insurance company's algorithm said that ten stiches were worth. So, the guy opened low and Mike left $1,000 on the table.

How times have changed, I can remember thinking. When I was a kid, stitches were something nobody wanted.

Today you can get paid for them.

MY WISDOM:

"It's a father's duty to give his son advice. Whether that advice is the right advice is another matter."

What the World Needs More of

*"There are no unwanted children, just unfound families." —*UNKNOWN

POPCORN IN HAND, I WAS KILLING time in the San Francisco airport, wandering between flights. I stopped in front of Gate 56 which was brimming with milling, excited people, each with a cheek-splitting grin on their face and a Christmas Eve look in their eyes.

Who were they waiting for, I wondered? The President? The Pope? Arnold Schwarzenegger? I decided to hang around and find out.

Suddenly the door to the exit ramp opened. The milling knots hushed; the silence was so deafening you could hear a baby hiccup. Which is exactly what I heard, as down the runway marched a smiling woman in a white nurses uniform, cradling a tiny bundle in her arms.

"May I present the Hildreth baby," she cooed to the crowd.

A shriek came from the back of the room. The crowd parted and from out of the knot charged a woman, her face as radiant as the setting sun. She held out her arms to the nurse and was handled the bundle in return. Then a gaggle of family members enveloped her, and the woman and her bundle disappeared into a sea of tears and hugs.

Then another starched woman emerged from the ramp. Same smile. Another bundle.

"May I present the McBride baby," she announced. Another delighted shriek, another parting of the Red Sea, followed by the handoff and the arrival of yet another gaggle of adoring family members.

"What's going on here"? I inquired of the ticket agent.

"A planeload of Korean orphans is meeting their new families," she beamed, her eyes glistening.

Whoa, I'd struck gold at Gate 56! Baby gold. An entire 747 filled with gold. What could I do but hunker down for the show.

And what a show it turned out to be, as Gate 56 turned into a veritable happiness factory. Babies poured out of that exit ramp like chocolate chip cookies out of my grandmother's oven, one baby after another, into the arms of their adoptive family.

If only those babies could talk. One minute I'm a lonely orphan, they'd say, with nothing but a tattered blanket and wet diaper to my name. No one to love, no one to love me. The next moment I'm being caressed by kind and loving eyes. My own private crib awaits, in my own blue or pink room filled with gifts and playthings and clean diapers.

I stood there, taking the scene in, as emotional as the parents themselves. Then I wandered from knot to glorious knot for what seemed to be hours, until I was mentally exhausted, spent like an old dollar bill.

Finally, the stream of bundles came to an end. The door to the exit ramp closed, the ladies in white disappeared, and the families slowly drifted away. And there I stood, alone at Gate 56, my plane long since departed for Minneapolis.

That scene opened my eyes to possibilities; possibilities that there can be a place for everyone in this world.

There can be a Gate 56 in everyone's life.

MY WISDOM:

"There is always someone, somewhere, who could

be part of your life if you let them."

After the Kids Leave Home

*"We must be willing to get rid of the life we've planned,
so as to have the life that is waiting for us."*
—JOSEPH CAMPBELL

Dictionary.com: DIVORCE: *noun,* a judicial declaration dissolving
a marriage in whole or in part.
My definition: DIVORCE: *noun,* a severed commitment.

TWO THINGS HAPPEN AS OUR KIDS grow up. They change. And
we change. And then, about the time our kids transition into adulthood, they pack up their worldly belongings and make the biggest
change of them all—they move out. And on. And, hopefully, up.

Which means the two adults that are left in the now-silent household must pull up a chair and make a handful of momentous decisions. What's next for the two of them? What needs to change?
What will fill the void of the kids being gone? Is the life they have
now as good as it gets?

And sometimes they decide their life *is* as good as it gets and
sometimes they decide that it isn't. And sometimes they do something about that decision and sometimes they don't. There isn't an
empty-nested father and mother who haven't asked themselves
those where-does-our-marriage-go-from-here questions after the
kids leave home.

Some call it a mid-life crisis. Others call it taking a pulse. Me? I call it taking inventory.

When inventory time happened in the days of our parents, they shrugged their shoulders and stayed where they were. A commitment was a commitment, I'm sure they said, and besides, the kids needed a place to call home when Thanksgiving and Christmas rolled around.

Those were the days when dads would fuss at their workbenches or mow the yard before heading to the golf course to trade stories with their buddies, while moms hunkered down over a bridge table or volunteered at the hospital.

"Just keepin' busy," they'd say with a weak smile.

But the times have changed, and along with the times, the meaning of the word "commitment" has changed too. For better or for worse, the word no longer means forever; rather it's more like for the near future. "Til death do us part" has also changed; "til death or divorce do us part" should be the revised vow.

Often, our lives are close to two-thirds over by the time the kids mosey on. Twenty-five more years, the statisticians tell us, before our lights are due to go out. Which means, if this is the case, that it makes little sense to spend those years with our hearts in a deep freeze when they could just as well be in the oven.

Happiness is too much fun.

What isn't too much fun though, is making a marriage commitment and then failing to keep it. That's because we know, when we break it, it won't endear us to some of the people we love the most, especially our kids. They want a home for the holidays, a home like it used to be with a mom and a dad and a link to the past.

Maybe marriages should be more like leases. Say, ten years with an option to renew. No more "till death do us part", but rather "till the year 2040". That way it will come as no surprise when inventory time comes around.

I took an inventory of my marriage when the kids left home and determined that twenty-five more years of what I had then wasn't in either of our best interests. That decision—to end the relationship—was not mutual, but it doesn't have to be. One of the two is all that it takes. Part of me still longs for one home with family photos plastered on every wall, mementos stuffed in every closet, and memories tucked in every drawer. A home with grand-children strewn around the living room floor like Fruit Loops on the kitchen table.

But it wasn't to be that way for me. And for us. I chose to pick a friend and a partner for the last phase of my life, not a holiday haven for my kids.

MY WISDOM:

"Nothing's the same after the kids leave home;

the hours you sleep, the company you keep,

or the reasons you weep."

PART THREE

GROWING OLD. 1996—TBD

A funny thing happened around the time I turned 75. My writing style changed and altered the way I approached stories. Sure, stories were still important, but the wisdom imbedded in them became more important than the story itself. I believe this happened as a result of my mentoring experiences over the preceding 30 years; experiences where the search for wisdom trumped the story. Stories are the teaser, wisdom is the prize.

My style was not the only thing that has changed over the year; my voice changed too. I wrote the stories in Parts One and Two (*Growing Up* and *Grown Up*) in my 50s, then filed them away because there was nothing else to do with them. Then, thirty years later, along came the idea for this book, and Parts Three and Four (*Growing Old* and *Looking Back*) were the natural extension. I wrote these last two Parts in my 80s when the passage of time and the influence of mentoring (and blogging too) had colored my writing. I hope you'll indulge me.

St. Andrews, Scotland

Grandson Tuck,
Todd, and Mary

Facilitating Business CEOs

See Mom, It's OK if My Academic Career Wasn't that Great

"Your attitude, not your aptitude, will determine your altitude." —ZIG ZIGLAR

OH, HOW I WISH MOM WERE still around so I could read the following letter to her. Maybe then she'd forgive me for bringing home so many mediocre grades over the years, especially in college. I think she'd pat me on the back and tell me that "getting high marks in school isn't the endgame anyway, it's really only the beginning game."

Anyway, here's the letter I'm talking about. A school principal in Singapore sent this to all the school's parents before the exams.

Dear Parents:

The exams of your children are to start soon. I know you are all anxious for your child to do well.

But please, remember that amongst the students who will be sitting for the exams there is an artist, who doesn't need to understand Math. There is an entrepreneur, who doesn't care about History or English literature. There is a musician, whose Chemistry marks won't matter. There's an athlete, whose physical fitness is more important than Physics. If your child does get top marks, that's great! But if he or she doesn't . . . please don't take their self-confidence and dignity away from them. Tell them it's OK, it's just an exam. They are cut out for much bigger things in life. Tell them, no matter what they score, you love them and will not judge them.

Please do this, and when you do, watch your children conquer the world. One exam or a low mark won't take away their dreams and talent. And please, don't think that doctors and engineers are the only happy people in the world.

With warm regards, Anonymous

Growing up, our education comes in many forms and from varied sources, and school is only one of those sources. Looking back, I learned as much from my paper route, my summer jobs, playing sports, and serving in the military, as I did in the classroom. Who knows, I might even have received As and Bs in a few of those experiences instead of the Bs and Cs that came from the classroom. I'm relieved to point out that my mom certainly wasn't alone in being disappointed in her son's educational achievements. I can only imagine how the moms of the following people must have felt, when their kids came home from school and said they were done with school and weren't going back . . .

Dropped out of high school: Richard Branson, Jennifer Lawrence, Walt Disney, Jay-Z, Leonardo DiCaprio, and Whoopi Goldberg.

Dropped out of college: Bill Gates, Oprah Winfrey, Albert Einstein, Steve Jobs, Ellen DeGeneres, and Princess Diana.

I know I disappointed Mom with my academic underperformance, and yes, I disappointed myself, especially in college. Dad never said much on the subject that I can remember, but I know how hard he worked to feed our family and send Chris and me to higher education. I'm sure he felt let down by watching his fun-loving son waste his money and his time underachieving for all those years. If I were my dad I know I would have felt let down.

The good news is that if Dad and Mom were still around, I think they'd give me at least a B in my life since my school days.

Maybe even an A-minus if they enjoyed this book.

MY WISDOM:

"It isn't how you begin the race that matters, it's

how you finish it."

Remembering the Old Coot

"Take care of all your memories, for you cannot relive them." —BOB DYLAN

I DON'T KNOW WHY PEOPLE MAKE fun of their in-laws. Personally, I've never had a bad one, which is hopefully what they would say about their son-in-laws. Especially this one.

But in-laws get old, and when they do, they can sometimes get cranky. I should know, today, at age 83, I'm quick to voice my displeasure, especially when people don't live up to my expectations. While my grandkids may think I'm lovable and fun, the guy on the phone who wants me to send money to Nigeria probably doesn't. He won't be dialing my number again anytime soon.

Speaking of old people, I'm reminded of Emmitt, Mary's late father.

It's 1983. Widowed for ten years, Emmitt called himself the "Old Coot," and no one disagreed—he was one. He did all the things that old coots do—grumble at waiters, order food not on the menu, and question every line item on the dinner check. I mean EVERY line item, and then tip ten percent. On the nose, as in one dollar and eighteen cents.

He was Billy Goat Gruff, growling at anyone who had the audacity to cross his bridge. He could be downright formidable too, especially toward those folks who were bent on selling him something, telling him something, or wanting to marry his only daughter, and so, in 1987, the same year the Simpsons made their first episode, I was the guy lucky enough to do that.

We soon became friends though, the Old Coot and I, and each year his visits to San Diego became more frequent. In the beginning he'd join us for Thanksgiving and Easter, but soon it was for the entire month of January (to beat Minnesota's cold and snow) and then July (to beat its mosquitoes and humidity). A jaunt here, a frequent flyer ticket there, and it wasn't long before the Old Coot was either comin', goin', or somewhere in between.

He slept in the small guest room too, not the big one with the mirrors, the TV, and the sitting room off the porch. "Big one's for snootpools," he'd grumble contentedly, before hunkering down in the single bed.

We celebrated the Old Coot's eighty-third birthday in 1994. He was still mowing his own yard (a quarter of an acre or so), shoveling his own snow (a couple of tons or so), and chauffeuring a lady coot around town.

The old coot died like we all want to go, quick and easy and in the right place. He took his last breath on his daughter's couch, watching the ten o'clock news, while the gin rummy cards were still warm.

It took a while to get over his passing, as it always does for people you love. But eventually the grieving subsided, and life was up to its old tricks again.

A year or so later I sliced my finger peeling potatoes. As she usually does at such times, Mary took charge.

"You need Bactine," she said, rolling her eyes as I snorted and cursed. "Dad always kept a bottle in the medicine cabinet in the guest bathroom. I'll bet it's still there."

We walked to the guest bathroom and opened the medicine cabinet. Sure enough, the Bactine was right where he'd left it. Right where it would be if he were still around.

Fast forward many years to 2013. We live in a different house now, in a different city and state, but still with a guest bathroom. And

Emmitt's Bactine is in that bathroom, resting safely in the medicine cabinet, right where it belongs.

Waiting patiently for me, the new old coot in the house, to use it in his name.

MY WISDOM:

"The most poignant memories come from the most ordinary stories."

Making a Case for Small Towns

*"The nice thing about living in a small town is that
when you don't know what you're doing, someone else
does."* —IMMANUEL KANT

IT WAS A CRISP FALL DAY in early October 1994 when our two-car
caravan crossed the California state line and breezed into Oregon.
We pulled off the road and snapped a picture with a "Welcome to
Oregon" sign in the background. Mary, our two dogs, Rudy and
Bogey, and Remi the cat, smiled for the camera, the bright afternoon sun mirroring our expectations of what life would be like in
our newly adopted state.

We were relocating from San Diego (pop. 2 million) to Bend,
(pop. 30,000). Prior to San Diego we'd lived in Minneapolis/St.
Paul (pop. 2.2 million). We knew we'd be in for a culture shock
with the move to a small town, so we were prepared for the worst.
Besides, the move we'd made four years earlier from staid Minnesota to crazy California had been a 7.0 on culture's Richter scale.
This one should be a coffee-cup rattler, or so we figured anyway.

Sure, we had concerns. Bend had no In and Out Burger for me
or Victoria's Secret for Mary. The ocean was now five *hours* away
instead of five *blocks*, so a lazy day on the beach would not be on the
calendar anytime soon. But Bend did have a snow-fed river mean-
dering through the center of town that, in the heat of summer, had

almost as many bodies tubing down it as the town had people. Bend also had its own TV station, a daily newspaper, and a main street dotted with shops that sold all kinds of touristy doodads. Most importantly, Bend had air fresher and cleaner than an Arctic night and tap water that tasted better than the stuff you buy in a bottle.

There is also one very important thing that Bend, like most small towns, did not have—an angry freeway crammed with cranky commuters. Rarely did you hear a horn honk in Bend, in exasperation or otherwise. (Which is still the case today, 25 years later). Meanwhile, a drive down Highway 5 in San Diego required ear plugs to keep the noise at a livable level.

Arriving in Bend slightly before dusk, our caravan stopped for gas before heading for the house we had purchased on a prior visit to town. At the gas station I bought (for 50 cents) a copy of *The Bulletin*, Bend's hometown newspaper. "Cougar Kills Llama in Sisters" (a neighboring town), the frontpage blared. As a previous subscriber to the *L.A. Times*, I saw that this kind of well-I'll-be-danged news was yet another sign that a small town would be the right place for us.

Even today, twenty-five years later, with a population nearing 100,000, Bend still has the feel of a small town. A wait of more than one change of a stoplight is uncommon, and road rage is something we see only on YouTube. The Op-ed page is the first page we look at when opening *The Bulletin*; we want to see who of our friends is complaining about something in their letters to the editor. The Obits is the second place we go.

There's also this time-wasting thing that exists in small towns. No matter where you go you can tack on fifteen minutes to your visit because you're going to run into a friend, neighbor, or co-worker there. The six degree of separation rule doesn't apply in small towns, it's more like two degrees.

There's another important benefit that comes from living in a small town: I have my doctor's email address. Furthermore, he responds to my emails first thing in the morning before he goes to work.

And that's not all . . .

- My dentist calls me at home after a tough session to make sure everything's OK.
- I go to the farmer's market and the people selling their goodies are the same people who grew them.
- We have a city park and a bandshell and there are lots of benches for sitting and thinking.
- We have a park with a horseshoe pit, and it's filled with old guys wearing suspenders and John Deere hats.
- I know a few of Bend's traffic cops by name. (I wish I didn't).
- The pace is also slower in small towns. Why, I'd be willing to bet there are significantly fewer psychiatrists per capita in Bend than there are in LA. The crowds are fewer, the DMV lines shorter, and I've never heard of someone's pocket being picked in Bend. Most people I know don't lock their doors during the day, but I'll bet they'd lock 'em up tight if they lived in Chicago or LA. And yes, housing is cheaper in a small town, and we have more mom and pop businesses than national chains, which means much of the money I spend in Bend, stays in Bend, which makes the spending of it more palatable.

But here's what I like the most about small towns: I walk down Main Street (yes, we have one of those) and approaching me is a man I don't know. He's a townie not a tourist, I can tell, from the way he's dressed and by his focused stride. He isn't looking in store windows.

We make eye contact. He smiles, then nods.

"Have a good day," he says as we pass.

"Back atcha," I reply.

And we both mean what we said.

MY WISDOM:

"Size doesn't matter. Location doesn't matter.

What matters is the people."

How to Make a Friend Without Opening Your Mouth

"The language of friendship is not words but meanings."
—HENRY DAVID THOREAU

FOR A DOZEN OR SO YEARS, Mary and I spent several weeks every winter in the Dominican Republic. The weather, the golf, and the friendly people of the city of La Romana had everything to do with that. In 2004 my son Todd and his wife, Robin, joined us for a long weekend over Thanksgiving, along with grandkids Tucker and Amanda. The Red Sox had just polished off the dastardly Yankees in a spine-tingling American League Championship Series, which meant that baseball fever was running high in the East Coast branch of the Schell family.

Given that backdrop, we decided to take in a Dominican grapefruit league, baseball game. We're not talking sandlot baseball here; the grapefruit league is made up of teams featuring players from the U.S. Major Leagues. Scouts cruise the stands; careers are at stake with every pitch.

Accompanying us to the game was a local Dominican family: Carolina the mother, and her two children, Manuel and Marciel. Manuel was five years old and Marciel eleven, while our Tucker was eleven and Amanda nine. Mary and I had befriended Carolina, an employee of the resort where we were staying.

The game was a barnburner with the La Romana Bulls dropping a heartbreaker in the ninth inning. Meanwhile, there was as much chatter, noise, and action in the stands as there was on the field. The Dominicans love their baseball!

Despite the nail-biting game, I couldn't take my eyes off the two girls, Marciel and Amanda. They were sitting with their mothers when the game began, sneaking sideways glances at each other, checking out whatever girls from divergent cultures find intriguing.

Remember, Marciel speaks Spanish and Amanda English. Marciel is black and hails from an all-black community, while Amanda is white, as is 95 percent of her hometown. Marciel's homeland is a developing country while Amanda's is the land of plenty. The two girls couldn't come from more divergent backgrounds.

By the time the ninth inning rolled around, Marciel and Amanda were sitting together, still not speaking, but exchanging nudges, smiles, and sideways looks. Language had taken a back seat.

Following the game, we convened at a pizza restaurant in La Romana where Amanda and Marciel sat side by side. Once the pizza was devoured, the two girls relocated to a balcony that overlooked a park where a crowd of Dominican children were playing basketball and hopscotch. Shoulder to shoulder the two girls looked on, quietly trading shy smiles.

Finally, it came time to call it a night. As our group exited the restaurant, my eyes were glued to the two girls. What would they do? How would they say goodbye? Amanda would be returning to the U.S. the following afternoon which meant, chances are, they'd never see each other again.

The adults exchanged hugs while Tucker gave Manuel the universal punch on the arm. Amanda and Marciel eyed each other and then, as my eyes glassed over, opened their arms and hugged. And I don't mean one of those "I'm so glad to see you, Aunt Millie" kind of hugs, either. It was more of a clung than a hug. Finally, they parted, exchanged embarrassed grins, got in their respective cars, and drove away.

The following morning, I brought up the incident at the breakfast table and related how I'd teared up when the two girls hugged. Amanda looked up from her Frosted Flakes.

"Grandpa," she said, rolling her eyes, "you make the biggest deal out of the littlest things."

She was right, of course. Except that that hug wasn't a little thing.

MY WISDOM:

"We need no common language to make

uncommon friends."

The Three-Day Rule for
Visiting Relatives

"Guests, like fish, get rotten after three days."
—BEN FRANKLIN

WHILE HER GRANDKIDS WERE GROWING UP in Minneapolis, Mom was living in Scottsdale, Arizona. As a result, our family didn't get to see her as often as we would have liked.

When she did come to visit, she'd buzz into town during the dog days of summer or maybe over the Christmas holidays. She'd fidget through a Little League baseball game in the summertime or shiver through a hockey game in the winter. Three days she would stay and never a day longer. She was not one to relive her years of raising kids—could I have had something to do with that?

"I don't want to wear out my welcome," she'd say briskly on her way out the door. And, needless to say, she didn't.

"But Mom," I'd plead as we'd get in the car for the drive to the airport, "couldn't you stay for at least one more day? Jim has a play-off hockey game and . . . ."

"Sorry, honey," she'd say, cutting me off. "I know that grandmas are supposed to get involved in their grandkids' lives, but I'm not that kind of a grandma," she'd conclude with a pat on my hand. "I have my own life to lead."

And that would be that. Back to Arizona she'd go.

Three days was all we could get out of her and then she'd head back to her life of teaching English as a second language, playing tournament bridge, and reading everything she could get her hands on. She missed Dad terribly, so she'd vowed to stay busy until the very end.

And so it's been for Mary and I; we make sure we don't wear out any welcomes either. It helps that one set of grandkids lives on the East Coast and the other in the Midwest, while we're way out west in the high desert country of Oregon. We've had our fill of humidity, mosquitoes, and winters from hell, the downsides of living where our Boston and Minneapolis grandkids grew up.

There are times when I envy those friends of ours who have chosen to live in the same town as their kids and grandkids. They're moments away from the action, available to babysit on Saturday night or house sit whenever called on, and always ready to hunker down in the kitchen for an afternoon chat. They never miss a soccer game, piano recital, or temper tantrum, and are an everyday fixture in the lives of their kids, and grandkids.

Sorry kids, but that's not the life for this grandparent. "I'm not that kind of a grandpa, I guess."

Today, my sons are grown and have become empty nesters themselves. While they were growing up, I exhausted every trick I knew to get them to adulthood safely, just as my parents did for me. But, as Mom had decided to do before me, I wouldn't be around to lick their wounds or bandage their sores, and I didn't take sides when the arguments began.

Today, Mary and I have the rest of our lives to live and so do our kids, and we don't want to be a burden to anyone. Heaven knows, our kids will have enough burdens of their own without having to shoulder ours.

Besides, my sons know everything that I know, at least where rearing a family, and making a living, and saying "I'm sorry" are concerned. Furthermore, I've ceded to them the right to pass along to their own kids whatever they've learned from me, including the best way to pop popcorn.

If they call, Mary and I will be there, but only for three days. We want them to be sad when we leave, not relieved.

MY WISDOM:

"I'd rather be on my kid's minds than in

their faces."

On a Pilgrimage; Returning Home

*"The magic thing about home is that it feels good
to leave, and it feels even better to come back."*
—UNKNOWN

EVERY BOY NEEDS A PLACE TO be alone, a place to forget homework, chores undone, and the girl in English class who won't give
him the time of day. Every boy needs a place to chase dragon flies
under soft summer skies. For me, that place was Waveland Golf
Course, a block away from our house. Waveland was, and still is,
a traditional, tree-lined, public golf course that's open to all and
provides four hours of pleasure in exchange for what it would cost
to buy a Coke and a hamburger at a private club.

Waveland is all trees, hills, and yawning ravines. The trees are
mostly oaks, and many were already adults back in 1901, the year the
course was built. The hills are never-ending and of the huff-and-puff
variety. The ravines are damp and smell of the musty leaves that
have been matted down by decades of rain and snow.

My friends and I would watch thunderstorms dance across Waveland's skies in the summertime and ski the cascading slopes of the
third and fifth holes in the winter. We'd exchange our latest secrets
as we walked Waveland's hills whilst trading visions of girlfriends,
current and fantasized. It was there we made plans for spending
our future riches, like the cattle ranch in Montana that Joe and I

would own someday, complete with bunkhouse and cook. Or was it a sheep ranch in Wyoming?

It was at Waveland that I learned to play golf. I learned the game from carrying someone else's bag and I learned it from lugging my own. I laughed while watching my friends screw up their game and I cried when I'd screw up my own.

In the summer, after dinner, I'd climb the fence surrounding Waveland, after the threat of waning light had chased the paying customers away. I'd play until the course disappeared in the evening's dusk, or until Tom, Waveland's ranger-on-a-mission, appeared on the horizon and chased me away.

I caddied for Waveland's finest, and I caddied for its worst. I watched otherwise responsible adults swoon, sweat, and swear in response to the errant flight of a golf ball. In the process, I grasped the vocabulary of golf while coining a few creative phrases of my own. And yes, I learned golf's gentlemanly etiquette; golf is a game where referees are not required because its players call fouls on themselves.

I left Des Moines after graduating from high school. College, the Air Force, a family, and a business career led me to greener pastures, to places far away from home. I rarely returned to Des Moines and never visited Waveland again.

Until, that is, the summer of 1977, twenty-three years after I said goodbye to Des Moines. I was on a pilgrimage that day, heading south on I-35, through the eye-numbing waves of corn that mark the drive from Minneapolis – where I lived at the time—to Des Moines. I'd planned the 250-mile drive to renew my acquaintance with Waveland; joining me was my eighteen-year old son, Jim.

We pulled into Waveland's parking lot and I gasped in surprise. The same brick clubhouse was there to greet me, having survived the years with little change. A sign here, a scoreboard there; a few new wrinkles on an old, familiar face.

Ghosts of the past loomed everywhere. The expansive oak tree that was the patriarch to all of Waveland's oaks still protected the eighteenth green. We entered the clubhouse; it still had the same musty aroma as the rug on my grandmother's porch. Inside, the oak-beamed party room that swayed to the tunes of Nat King Cole on Saturday nights in the 1940s and 50s looked and felt the same, albeit a little more tired.

An out-of-town check for $33.77, accepted without identification, purchased two green fees, two pull carts, and one embroidered Waveland golf cap for me. We were quickly on the first tee as a light drizzle began to fall. My arms were speckled with goose bumps; it was good to be back.

The drizzle kept the unfaithful at home, which gave Jim and me time to analyze every hole and anticipate every shot. And for me to catch my breat h from climbing Waveland's hills, they seemed to have steepened over the years.

Four hours after we began, the afternoon came to an end. Jim congratulated me with a "great putt, Dad" after my downhill ten-footer on the eighteenth hole went rattle, then klunk, for a par.

We exchanged hugs; then Jim walked, and I floated, up the hill from the eighteenth green to the parking lot. I could tell he'd enjoyed the day almost as much as I had. I barely noticed the climb for the lump in my throat.

We passed the old oak, its leaves damp with drizzle, still quietly protecting Waveland from harm. "I'll be back," I promised the old tree, in a voice loud enough that only the two of us could hear.

MY WISDOM:

"Childhood memories are the best memories,

especially when you can share them with

your kids."

When a Memento Becomes a Keepsake

"Not everything worth keeping has to be useful."
—CYNTHIA LORD

THE PHONE CALL FROM CHRIS CAME late at night. "I just got off the phone with the Arizona State Highway Patrol," she said softly. "Mom was in an automobile accident." She paused, her forced breathing foretelling what was coming next.

"She's with Dad now," she continued, a catch in her voice. "I'll bet they're thrilled to be back together again."

For those of us who live far away from our parents, in the back of our mind we know this phone call will eventually come. Fifteen years earlier the call had come from Mom to tell me that Dad, freshly retired at age 64, had collapsed in the buffet line of the golf course where he was playing. He was gone before he hit the floor.

With the latest phone call, Chris and I began the delicate unwinding of our mother's life. Several weeks later, in the summer heat of Arizona, we gingerly sorted through her one-bedroom condo, picking through her lifetime of belongings. We sold the impersonal stuff; her aging Ford Thunderbird, the grandfather clock that needed fixing, the creaky furniture that seemed out of place in a contemporary Arizona condo. Her beloved books went to the public library to be read by others. We knew she'd like that.

And then there was the personal stuff; the reminders, the mementos, the keepsakes, the leftovers that marked 79 years of Mom's life. That personal stuff included packets of pictures now tinged in yellow; framed photos of Mom and Dad doing the chores on the farms where they grew up, of Mom's uniformed brother Bill, who'd left Blakesburg, Iowa for the Naval Academy and went on to become a much-decorated, four-star admiral in the U.S. Navy.

There were also bundles of grayed letters from relatives and friends that she'd saved along with a newspaper clipping announcing her hole-in-one at the Perry, Iowa municipal golf course. Dad never had one, a fact which Mom would not let him forget.

She lived an organized, minimal life, a life where everything had its place. If it didn't do something meaningful, Mom didn't own it. She was a survivor of the Great Depression, which meant that everything she purchased must have a purpose, a reason to exist. There were no irrelevant knick-knacks sitting on tables or nailed to the walls, no boxes filled with junk or surprises. There would be no mysteries unearthed as we sifted through Mom's lifetime accumulation of stuff.

Well, except for one. There was this buckeye. A UPS brown, shiny, oval shaped, buckeye.

A buckeye is a brown nut that grows on the official state tree of Ohio. It's also better known as the nickname of the Ohio State University football team. Chris and I could remember seeing that shiny brown buckeye resting in a small jewelry box inside the chest of drawers in Mom's bedroom when we were growing up. There it remained for as long as we could remember, alongside her earrings, bracelets, and pins. Dad's wedding ring was in that jewelry box too, where Mom could see it every morning when she reached for her wristwatch.

Despite the fact we'd seen that buckeye for all those years, we'd never asked her what it meant or why she kept it. It was yet another in the long line of questions that kids don't ask their parents until it's too late. Only Mom knew the story behind that buckeye, and she wasn't telling, it's secret would be forever lost. I'm sure she and

Dad were cracking up, watching us as we scratched our heads over that shiny brown buckeye.

Fast forward twenty years to 2009. It's a frigid, blustery, weekend day in Bend; one of those do-nothing winter days when you light a fire in the fireplace and have no intention of venturing outside. Thanks to the internet however, it's difficult to be bored for too long, no matter how inclement the weather might be. And so, in lieu of hunkering down with a book, on an impulse I decided to drop in on Ancestry.com and see what I could learn.

In case you've never done the Ancestry.com thing, if you click on enough links and ask enough questions, you'll discover a digital persona – an actual person—out there, somewhere in cyberspace, who is familiar with the region of the country you're interested in. For me, that region was southeastern Iowa, and included the community of Blakesburg, where Mom and her five siblings grew up. Blakesburg, I learned from the unseen digital guru, had its own newspaper dating back to the early 1900s and, miracle of miracles, you could sort on a name and if that name was mentioned in the local newspaper, up would pop the article. Since my grandfather's surname was eminently sortable (Schoech), I dug in. Let the search begin.

A half an hour later, up popped a 1925 article in the *Blakesburg Excelsior* that informed its readers that Joe Schoech had decided that carrying a hog's tooth in his pocket was not going to cure his rheumatism. (Arthritis, to you young'uns). In its place, he'd carry a new talisman, one more likely to resolve his rheumatic condition.

He would, the *Excelsior* informed us, from this point forward, carry a buckeye in his pocket.

Eureka, I'd hit the mother lode! The answer to the unsolved mystery. That shiny, buffed-to-a-sheen buckeye was our grandfather's cure for arthritis. How could medical science have overlooked such a discovery?

Today, that buckeye rests comfortably in Chris's Denver home, dependent on her safekeeping, still every bit as shiny and brown as it was the day we found it.

Waiting to be passed on to Chris's kids, who won't have to wonder what it is or why it's still around.

MY WISDOM:

"One hundred buckeyes may be a bushel, but one

buckeye is a story."

Without This One Thing, Your Marriage Will Never Work

"Marriage is an alliance entered into by a man who can't sleep with the window shut, and a woman who can't sleep with the window open."
—GEORGE BERNARD SHAW

"HONEY," MARY HAS BEEN KNOWN TO ask, "what would you like for dinner?"

"Meat loaf," I've been known to reply.

"Hmmm," she's been known to respond, "that doesn't sound good to me. Let's have spaghetti instead."

"Sure, that sounds awesome, honey. Now why didn't I think of that?"

What was happening here, of course, was that I was compromising, because, in the grand scheme of things, what we'd have for dinner that night didn't matter that much.

Speaking of which, here's another exchange in much the same vein.

"Honey," she'd say, "I want to live in Tucson six months a year. I'm tired of being cold."

"Whoa," I'd croak, clutching my throat. In the grand scheme of things, moving to Tucson for six months did matter. As in hugely. "We . . . we . . . need to work out a compromise here."

Well, I'm happy to report, we did work out a compromise on that Tucson proposal, just like we did on the spaghetti. We now live in Tucson six months a year.

Did I cave? Well, not entirely, Rather, I compromised

One must first understand that, after twenty years of being a small business owner, Mary sold her business in the summer of 2017. She had, as she put it, "milked the cow long enough." It was time for someone else to take her place on the stool.

The upsides of those twenty years were that she'd had a good run, in the process making a significant contribution to our retirement fund.

The downsides? She'd been her company's chief conflict negotiator and problem-solver, negotiating and resolving the unending stream of headaches that go along with owning a business and being the boss. She had a change coming to her life. She'd earned it.

Meanwhile, while she'd been busy resolving those headaches, I'd been busy having fun. Well, my version of fun anyway, no matter what you call the kind of community-building stuff that I'd been doing over those years. The point was, that if I didn't enjoy whatever it was I was doing, I didn't do it. Mary didn't have that option.

Which translates to, in effect: I owed her big time for the past twenty years.

Oh yes, there's one other reason why I owed her big time. Our move from San Diego to Bend twenty-five years earlier had been my idea—she'd come along for the ride. She'd been content living in San Diego, or at least more content than I.

This background accounts for the reason I compromised on the move to Tucson in the winter. I loved Bend from the get-go while she liked Bend. Meanwhile, she loved Tucson from the get-go while I liked it.

Sounds like the opportunity for compromise to me.

As with all successful partnerships, Mary and I have our differences—different needs, different politics, different ways of resolving conflict. While resolving those differences requires plenty of old-fashioned patience and understanding, the result is a partnership that's worked for both of us, over our thirty-four-years-and-counting marriage.

Warm or cold. Republican or Democrat. Dog or cat. There are dozens (hundreds?) of gaps in needs and wants that threaten all partnerships, and it's compromise that bridges those gaps.

You could say that Mary "won" when we made the decision to become snowbirds over the winter, and you'd be right. But I didn't lose.

If Tucson makes her happy, then I've won too.

MY WISDOM:

"It isn't about what's best for me. It's about what's

best for us."

The Day My Doctor Told Me
He'd Made a Mistake

"General anesthesia is so weird. You go to sleep in one room, then four hours later you wake up in a totally different room. Just like in college." —ROSS SHAFER

IT'S OCTOBER OF 2011 AND I was in the Recovery Room of Bend's St. Charles Medical Center, snoozing away like a tired puppy. I'd been on the receiving end of two hours of back (L4, L5) surgery, and was off somewhere in lala land, the anesthesia doing its job.

I can vaguely remember my deep sleep morphing into that stage of grogginess that is the next step of the post-surgery process. I can barely recall my eyelids fluttering, as my eyes struggled to come into focus. What I can remember however, clear as a bell, was the shadow that was hovering over me as I opened my eyes.

"Hi, Jim, Doctor Larsen here," the shadow said. Even in my stupor I recognized the man. He was my surgeon, the guy who'd just finished carving up my back with an X-Acto knife.

I shook my head, but the cobwebs still clung. "Urg, gloop," I said to the shadow that was Dr. Larsen.

"Jim, I made a mistake," he continued, his eyes staring into mine.

Whammo, so much for lala land, I was wide awake now. If you ever need to wake up in a microsecond, have your surgeon tell you he made a mistake.

"Say . . . say that again," I stammered, trying to sit up in the gurney. I couldn't budge as the shadow's hand was pressed hard against my chest, making sure I didn't move. Oh yes, I now have a freshly reconstructed vertebra. I almost forgot.

"Jim, I said I made a mistake during the surgery, but don't worry, I've fixed it. You'll be fine," Dr. Larsen went on, then added the word "tomorrow" to the end of that sentence.

"You mean I'm not OK today?" I replied, my doped-up head spinning with possibilities.

"You'll be fine today, too, Jim" Doctor Larsen replied, with a grin. "But maybe you'll be a tad uncomfortable. You're going to have to remain flat on your back for the next 24 hours."

"Whafor?" I sputtered. I was ready to go home.

"Jim, your spinal cord is surrounded by spinal fluid. That spinal fluid is inside what we call a dura mater sac. I slightly tore it in the course of your surgery, and it leaked a little, but I've sewn it back up. Everything's fine, except, like I said, you'll need to remain in bed, flat on your back, for the next 24 hours." He glanced at his watch like people do when they're late for something, which he probably was. Docs are always late for something, mostly because they spend too much time answering stupid questions from patients like me.

"Oh, that's all? Just 24 hours?" I said, a comment I would find incredibly stupid over the following 1,440 minutes.

1,440 minutes is a lot of minutes when you're lying flat on your back counting holes in the ceiling tile. Especially, at night when the hospital goes to sleep and there's nothing to do but lie on your back and feel sorry for yourself.

If you ever need to stretch 24 hours into a week, I know a surefire way to help you do that. Try lying flat on your back for that many hours and staring at the ceiling. I guarantee it will be the longest f#@&*ing seven days of your life, and you'll be talking dirty to that stupid ceiling by the time those 24 hours are over. I should know. I was. And did.

But hey, my torn dura mater sac healed, and eight years later, here I am, writing a story about it. Which means, like Mom used to say, all's well that ends well.

But wait, in addition to my sordid memory of that experience, there's more to this story. Here are the four shocking words that I heard from my doc that I will always remember...

"I. Made. A. Mistake."

Think about it. When was the last time you heard a doctor tell you he or she made a mistake? Never, I'll bet. I'm not surprised—I never have either, before or since.

But I'd bet you dollars to donuts that docs have made plenty of mistakes on you and I at one time or another over those years. Last I heard, they're human, and we all know that one of the primary reasons that humans are put on this earth is to screw things up and then not tell anyone about it.

I've since learned the reason why Dr. Larsen 'fessed up. A 2010 study by the University of Michigan and Brigham and Women's Hospital concluded that when doctors apologize for their mistakes, malpractice lawsuits can often be avoided. In other words, admitting your mistakes is good for their business. Makes sense to me.

In fact, there are people out there who make their living helping docs apologize for their mistakes. Sorry Works! is a 501 (c) 3 nonprofit which is, in its own words, a *"nonprofit dedicated to disclosure and apology for medical errors."* How weird is it that an organization can exist that provides coverups for people's mistakes? (If only Richard Nixon had known). But I get it, as a direct result of Dr. Larsen's apology, I never considered suing either the doc or the hospital for my poor, torn, dura mater sac. Like most rational humans, I like it when people say they're sorry when they're wrong. Makes me forgive 'em.

This was the first and only time I've heard a "professional" tell me that he (or she) made a mistake. Two other categories of professionals come to mind when I say this: attorneys and CPAs, especially those CPAs who do your taxes. I know, yes, I KNOW, that there must have been plenty of times over the 60 or so years since I entered adulthood that the attorneys and CPAs I've hired have messed something up.

How could they not? It isn't easy what they do for a living—there are a gazillion rules, regulations, and laws they must consider every time they arrive at a conclusion. They can't be right all the time. They just can't.

I'm the first to admit that professionals have a tough row to hoe; if I were a doc, attorney, or CPA, I'd be the number one customer of Sorry Works! As my wife will attest, making mistakes is an integral part of my MO; nary a day goes by when I don't make a bushel of them.

There are three kinds of professionals, as I've since come to realize: crummy ones, good ones, and excellent ones. Most of the docs I've had fall in the excellent category, and I respect and appreciate what they do, both for me and for mankind.

Which leads me to a lesson I learned a long time ago: I need to be nice to the people who know how to solve life's problems that I can't solve.

I need *them* a lot more than they need *me*.

MY WISDOM:

"When you make a mistake, the first thing to do is

to admit that you're wrong. The second thing

is to fix it."

Meaningful Work Makes for a Meaningful Life

"For, in the end, it is impossible to have a great life unless it is a meaningful life. And it is very difficult to have a meaningful life without meaningful work."
—JIM COLLINS

CHAD WAS A LONG-TIME FRIEND AND a down-the-road Minnesota neighbor. A warm and caring man, his father and mother had passed away when he was in his early thirties, leaving him financially secure. He then determined there was no compelling reason to pursue a working career, so he hung it up and chose family and golf instead.

Chad was one of those shadowy people that we working stiffs would see strolling around the golf course on weekday afternoons. For twenty-five years he was the envy of most of the people who knew him, including me. We're working and stressed and hunched in our office, we thought, while he's playing and carefree and wandering a golf course.

We wished we were him.

Fast forward another twenty-five years to age fifty-five. Chad and I are hunkered down over a beer, when out of the blue he turns to me and says "Jim, I envy you. You've built a business. Enjoyed a career. Mentored people. Created something. Watched it grow. You've left your mark."

Did I hear him right? He envies me? He, who's been traveling the world and golfing on weekdays and always around when his kids came home from school? He envies me, who's been selling his soul to the bankers and stewing about meeting payroll and shortchanging my kids by working on weekends?

I reminded him he had created something as well – a family. A good one too. He'd helped it to grow and prosper. For sure, he'd left his mark.

"OK, yeah, I know," he nodded, his eyes downcast. "But family isn't enough, I know now. I've needed something more, especially now that the kids are gone."

And from that conversation I came to understand; golf may be a stroll in the park on a warm summer day, but it doesn't leave anything distinguishable behind it. Nothing to be remembered by. Nothing that made a difference in anyone's life but your own. Sure, families are important, but as the years go by, the kids grow up, then leave home and move on. They're busy living their lives and we should be busy living ours. We should be around to help them when they need us, but they have their life to live and we have ours.

What Chad had learned was that there needs to be something in our lives to keep us engaged as we grow older. Something to keep us energized, passionate, and above all else, something that makes us "relevant", within our neighborhood, our community, or our world. Something that can make life purposeful, after the kids have left home.

Our work gives us meaning at the same time it provides us with a venue to make a difference. It's more than just a way to pay the bills, it's an essential part of the human spirit, right up there with play and love. Without all three in our life, something is missing.

Shortly after our conversation, Chad went back to work, kicking off a second career as a financial advisor. As I write, he just turned eighty.

And still goes to work every day.

MY WISDOM:

"Work gives us relevance and relevance gives us meaning. Life without meaning is not a full life."

The Day You Learn You're Not Bulletproof Anymore

"The greatest wealth is health." —VIRGIL

IT WAS JUNE 20, 2003, 6:00 o'clock in the morning. I was in my home office when it happened. I can remember it as if it were yesterday, I was sitting in front of my computer with a fiery sunrise raging on Mt. Jefferson, as seen through my office window. I glanced at the still-snowclad mountain as it reflected the early morning sun. A day couldn't be shaping up any better than this one, I can remember thinking. I'd work on a book I was writing in the morning and then head to the golf course following lunch. A half day of meaningful work and a half day of enjoyable play; life at age sixty-seven couldn't get much better than this.

I'd kicked off this later-in-life writing career thirteen years earlier, which meant I knew how to make my keyboard sing. I was doing my best Van Cliburn imitation when, out of nowhere, a teaspoon of liquid flooded my right eye, as if someone had squirted pancake syrup on my eyeball.

"WTF?" I said to Baggie, my favorite mutt. She wagged her tail and smiled at the attention. If you're a dog parent, you know the look.

My vision blurred. I tried to blink the syrup away. No luck.

I rubbed my eye with my sleeve, like you do in the morning when trying to rub the night's remnants away. Still no change.

I shook my head once, then again. No dice. Whatever was happening was scaring me. I had the sick feeling we've all experienced that these new and strange bodily symptoms weren't in my best interest.

I closed my left eye – the one without the pancake syrup – and the right one couldn't make out the words on the monitor. I could see the brightness of the screen, but the details were fuzzy.

The rest of the day was a blur, if you'll pardon the expression. I made a beeline to an eye doctor who, in turn, referred me to a retina specialist. By dinnertime I knew the meaning of the term "wet macular degeneration." Look it up if you're, uh, fuzzy on the translation, but it basically means your vision in that eye is gone, as in it's toast. Forever.

I also learned one other lesson that day; one we all discover at some point in our lives.

I wasn't bulletproof anymore.

Healthwise, I'd been a walking gold mine up to this point. I was still upright while several of my friends weren't. I played golf, traveled, and was making a difference in people's lives. My life was chugging along on script; I was just busy enough. I was doing things I wanted to do, not things I needed to do. My days were about as good as an aging elder's days can get.

Before this eyesight thing took place, healthcare amounted to an annual checkup followed by a green light. "Your vital signs are good," the doc would say, "feel free to do whatever you want, although you might want to give rugby and skydiving a pass." This eye thing, however, would open a Pandora's box of little, aggravating stuff over the next couple of years, like hip replacements, back problems, and failing rotator cuffs.

Those things can be fixed.

A damaged retina can't.

By the following day I was 95% blind in the syrupy eye and would remain that way for the rest of my life. Meanwhile, the good eye was working just fine. Surprising as it may sound, losing one eye is little more than a minor inconvenience. Sure, you lose depth perception—you won't be shagging fly balls in centerfield anymore. And yes, you'll need to crane your neck when changing lanes, which makes driving at night especially dicey. Plus, you squint a lot, but that's about it for the downsides of being down to one eye.

Well, except for one great big, huge, major, frightening, downside. You're now one eye away from being blind.

My retina doc, who is now *the most* important non-relative in my life, has never mentioned the word "blind" in my presence. Furthermore, thanks to one of the many miracles of modern medicine, he'll hopefully never have to. I get an injection in the good eye (yes, a needle stuck in it) every four weeks which has, for the past sixteen years, kept the eye bogeyman at bay.

It's no secret that there's a price to be paid for getting old. That price is our health. We can toil religiously to slow the decline, but we can't stop aging from taking its relentless toll. Sure, we can slow it down by minding our diet, exercising our body, and keeping our mind active, and all the other good things the experts recommend.

But our days of getting up in the morning and feeling like a million bucks are gone. Now it's more like a hundred bucks. On good days maybe a thousand, on bad days fifty cents.

Now don't get me wrong, aging has some benefits. Wisdom is the biggest of the batch, but so are friends, family, and, hopefully, a feeling of accomplishment for a life well led. There's also a sense of contentment for some of us, a feeling that we've done the best we can do, which, when you think about it, is *all* we can do.

Most of all, assuming our health cooperates, getting old provides an opportunity to chase the dreams we haven't had the time to chase until now. Now that we've earned the wisdom that comes with age, we can do what folks like Jimmy Carter (who is alive but suffering as I write this) are doing around the world, or what some of our local heroes are doing in our own community.

The world is our palette at this time in our life, and we are the artist. We can paint any picture we please.

MY WISDOM:

"Growing old may not be for sissies, but it's not for quitters either. There's always something more we can do."

Losing A True Friend

"Many people will walk in and out of your life, but only true friends will leave footprints in your heart."
—ELEANOR ROOSEVELT

THE PHONE CALL CAME FROM JOE, one of my game-playing buddies growing up. "Jim, I hate to be the bearer of bad news, but Dunk isn't with us anymore. He died in his sleep last night."

Remember Dunk? The kid who shared a tent with me the night we tasted our inaugural beer? The same kid who scrawled the F-Word on Mom's to-do-list board, after I beat him in ping pong? The two of us had been best friends throughout high school and remained good friends as life led us in different directions.

Today, two years after Dunk's passing, hardly a day goes by when I don't think of him, despite the fact that, over the fifty-five years since we graduated from college, we'd only seen each other a couple of dozen times over the years. He was still living in Des Moines when he died, while I've rambled in and out of a dozen or so cities and towns over my lifetime. We'd share a beer when I'd come home for a high school reunion or visit my parents, and as soon as we took the first sip the years would peel away, and we were high school pals all over again.

And yet, I miss him like I'd seen him every day. As much as anyone I've ever lost, parents excluded. The world is emptier without Dunk being a phone call away. And lonelier.

Now, with him gone, I've also lost my connection to home. Which means, goodbye forever to Des Moines, there's no reason to return anymore.

I've often wondered why I felt so strongly about losing Dunk. Then recently, I stumbled on a blog post that featured the musings of Aristotle. It's amazing how much we can learn from someone who'd be 2,000 years old if he were still alive today.

The subject of the blog post was Aristotle's thoughts on "friends." According to him, there are three kinds of friendships:

Utility Friendship: Aristotle calls a Utility Friendship a friendship of benefit, maintained because the two friends *benefit* from the exchange—a business or working relationship, for instance. When the utility of the relationship ends, so does the friendship.

Pleasure Friendship: This friendship Aristotle dubbed a friendship of enjoyment, where two friends find *pleasure* in their relationship. Examples include partners in a romantic relationship, or members of a sports team or book club. Similar to a Utility Friendship, the Pleasure Friendship lacks permanence, when the pleasure wanes or disappears, the friendship ends.

True Friendship: Finally, Aristotle calls this the Friendship of the Good. It's based on similar virtues, ethics, and mutual appreciation. That mutual appreciation, in turn, features the presence of empathy and caring between the two true friends. Empathy and caring transcend time, Aristotle goes on to say, which is why a True Friendship lasts forever.

The Utility and Pleasure Friendships, Aristotle concluded, are not necessarily lesser friendships; they fill a void at the time they take place. But the lack of depth limits their quality, which means that as soon as the benefits and pleasures subside, the friendship ends.

Not so for True Friendships. True Friends, Aristotle says, are "a single soul dwelling in two bodies." True friends are like family, he concludes, which answered my question about the depth of my feelings for Dunk.

When he passed, I lost more than a friend. I lost the brother I never had.

MY WISDOM:

"Our childhood friends are our most

revered friends."

A Word to the Medical Profession: Err on the Low Side

"Death is life's change agent. It clears out the old to make way for the new." —STEVE JOBS

IT WAS AUGUST 2017, A MONTH before my 80th birthday. I'd just taken my annual physical—my protein level had spiked, as shown by a blood test. "A potential symptom of bone marrow cancer," the doc had said gravely, which resulted in me being hastily dispatched to a cancer specialist. This would be my second "C experience" of the decade: eight years prior I'd been diagnosed with prostate cancer. Beat the bugger too, thanks to modern medicine and a robot that removed the offending gland.

I'd need a biopsy, my cancer doc said, which entailed the removal of a small chunk of bone from the back of my pelvis. While he was digging, I asked him the question every cancer doc has heard a zillion times over his career.

"So, Doc, what're the chances I really have bone marrow cancer?"

"Hmmm," he replied, between prods. "I'd say about . . . 80%."

Now if I was a cancer doc and was asked that question, I'd err on the low side. And he WAS a cancer doc and if 80% was erring on the low side, then I didn't want to know what the high side was. Displaying a rare flash of forbearance, I kept my mouth shut and returned home after the biopsy was finished. Two weeks it would take for the lab results to come back, the doc had said.

Two weeks of waiting for the shoe to drop.

That would be two weeks from hell, or so I thought on the drive home. Except that it wasn't. Somehow my brain shifted into neutral, and what I thought would be two weeks of misery turned out to be little more than a minor inconvenience. On par with a toothache.

Oh, I researched bone marrow cancer (four to five years life expectancy) and discussed our options with Mary. Then we went about our business as if those 14 days was just another two weeks in our life. Somehow, I suspect, my innate optimism kicked in and instead of assuming I'd be one of the 80%, my mind opted for the 20% instead.

Besides, I'd had a good run if the shoe *were* to drop. Heck, I was living on borrowed time anyway—my dad passed of a stroke at age 64 which, DNA wise, doesn't bode well for me, his only son. Besides, the life expectancy of a U.S. male at the time was 79, which meant I was into my bonus years.

There'd be no complaints from me if I was one of the 80%. I'd had a fair shake.

At Mary's request, we reviewed my bucket list. Not surprisingly, nothing was on it. If given a month to live, I'd probably do a lot of the same stuff I'm currently doing. Sure, we'd call the kids and they'd come to town, then we'd play some golf and swap some stories. Mary and I might take a golf trip somewhere as we wound things down, and I'd eat all the chocolate I could get my hands on.

For me, at this point in my life, death is not *that* big a deal. While I'm not looking forward to it, there's an element of mystery about what happens next. According to Steve Jobs' sister (who was with him at his deathbed), his last six words were, "Oh wow, oh wow, oh wow," which leads me to believe he was seeing something enticingly cool on the other side. (Maybe someday we'll have an app for it).

Death is such a small part of the living experience anyway, it is barely one pixel on a wide-angle screen. One day you're here, the next day you're not.

John Lennon once said that he was not afraid of death, because he simply didn't believe in it. "It's just getting out of one car and into another," he concluded. The fact that we don't know what kind of car he'd be getting into only added to the mystery.

Besides, we aren't going to be remembered for the way we died, but rather for the way we lived.

MY WISDOM:

"Death is a small price to pay for life, which,

in turn, is the best deal in town."

When You Realize You're Not Quite as Good as You Used to Be

"Old age is always fifteen years older than I am."
—OLIVER WENDELL HOLMES

"HOW WAS YOUR DAY TODAY, HONEY"? Mary asked, as I slumped in the door after a long day at my version of work.

"I think I'm losing it," I grumbled, making my way to the refrigerator. There was a beer in my immediate future.

"What's '*it*'?" she replied, handing me the bottle opener I was having trouble finding. I opened a beer and took a long swig.

"My presentation skills. I spoke to the Rotary Club today. I sucked."

"Oh, poor man," she cooed, patting me on the head. She doesn't like it when I feel sorry for myself. "What was it that sucked so much?"

"A couple of times I got off on a tangent. Then, when I'd try to get back where I was, I'd get lost," I replied, followed by another swig.

"But that's . . ." she began.

"And that's not all," I went on, gathering steam. "Several times I couldn't remember a word I needed to complete a sentence." Swig again.

"Arghhh," I added, remembering the audience's pained silence as I searched for the right word. And then, wouldn't you know it, I came up with the wrong one.

"Well, still . . . "

"And then," I couldn't be stopped now, "someone asked a question from the back of the room. I couldn't hear what the guy said, so I had to ask him to speak louder."

"Maybe you need new hearing aids," she said. I wasn't sure if she was joking, as I was already on my third pair. Those babies cost an arm and a leg.

"Anyway," I said, leaning back in my chair, like I do when I'm about to wax philosophical, "My presentation skills are barely tolerable. No, make that totally useless.

"That's it for my public speaking career," I said. As if I ever had a speaking career."

Final swig, which marked the end of my alcohol consumption for the night. One's my limit; even my drinking sucks.

"Public speaking isn't for old people," I concluded, walking out of the kitchen and heading for the safety of my Barcalounger. "It's time to move on. Golf, here I come."

On the drive home from the fateful Rotary presentation, I'd started thinking of all the other things that weren't a good fit for old people either. Anything that requires solid hearing, eyesight, memory, complexity, and/or immediacy come to mind. In case you're wondering, that Rotary speech wasn't the first time I'd noticed my suckiness, but it *was* the first time I'd publicly embarrassed myself. Well, the first time I'd noticed, anyway.

Losing the physical stuff is tough enough, but the silent sapping of one's cognitive competence is the hardest pill to swallow. Why, even balancing a checkbook, something I've been doing once a month for sixty years (that's 720 times), was becoming a chore. Sure, I eventually balance the damn thing, but the close-enough number keeps getting bigger.

Several days after the Rotary conversation, my monthly issue of Atlantic magazine arrived. Yes, I'm one of those people who still have magazine subscriptions. Don't judge.

One of the articles spoke to the topic of declining abilities caused by aging and the impact it has on the person doing the declining.

In the article, the writer, one Arthur Brooks, notes that the waning of ability in people as they age is "especially brutal psychologically." Little does Brooks know, I'll bet he's not even 80 yet. Just wait, buddy.

Brooks went on to explain to his readers that "if your profession requires mental processing speed or significant analytic capabilities, a noticeable decline is going to set in earlier than you imagine." For me, and for others I know, that noticeable decline began sometime around the time I turned 75. Beware, I would say, to those of you who are 74. Don't say I didn't warn you.

I found partial redemption later in Brook's article when he revealed that "teaching (aka mentoring, one of my favorite things to do) is an ability that decays very late in life, a principal exception to the general pattern of professional decline over time." That explains why, I assume, you see so many college professors over 70 (even 80!) in the classrooms these days. Those old codgers can still get the job done.

Stop me if I've said this before, but Brooks' mention of teaching (aka mentoring) has helped to buoy my otherwise flagging spirits about aging. His statement outlines that single, solitary thing where, instead of a noticeable decline, us old folks can witness an improvement.

Which is why mentoring is, today, my favorite thing to do.

MY WISDOM:

"Getting old can't be stopped; but acting old can

be slowed down by staying relevant."

The Luck of the Draw

"Don't let thinking of yesterday take up too much of today." —WILL ROGERS

IT'S 2019, AND IN ANOTHER OF life's small-world coincidences, I ran into Mike, the son of a friend from my pre-1990 Minnesota years. Mike and his wife Kelly, like so many other outdoor-loving people, had gravitated to Bend for the quality of life our community offers. They'd been in town for a year before we ran into each other.

Shortly after learning they were in town, I met with Mike and we traded family and Minnesota stories over a beer. I'd played softball against his dad, Tom, who'd died unexpectedly at the young age of 62. A former college and minor league baseball player, Tom didn't drink, smoke, or carouse. If anyone deserved to live 'til a ripe old age, Tom did.

And yet, he didn't.

In earlier chapters you'll recall my friend Dunk. An All-American football player in college, Dunk had no appreciable vices and was practicing law right up to the day he was diagnosed with brain cancer. His parents had lived into their nineties and, in a logical world, he should have, too.

And yet, he didn't either.

On the drive home after my beer with Mike, a wave of nostalgia engulfed me. Nostalgia seems to strike frequently these days; I'm in that stage when the world becomes just a little bit lonelier with each passing month. It's rare that thirty days go by when I don't hear of a friend that's gone, or is soon to be gone, or is shackled at home for health-related reasons. Meanwhile, I'm out having a beer with their sons and daughters.

I pulled into the garage, switched off the engine, and took a deep breath, a smidge of guilt fogging my thoughts. Why should I be the gainfully engaged survivor, while my friends are no longer around? Sure, I've done a decent job of taking care of myself, but I'm not the finest physical specimen that ever graced the face of the earth. Also, my dad died at age 64, which means my genes, at least on his side, are suspect. And, if that isn't enough, I've survived a brush with prostate cancer and a messy automobile accident in my later years. OK, so I haven't gone through the proverbial nine lives yet, but I'm working on them.

Yet here I am, 82 years old with my sights set on 90. I'm happy, healthy (relatively speaking), and looking forward to whatever tomorrow will bring. Mary and I are planning a golf trip to Ireland this summer, where we'll walk its storied courses for ten straight days, seven miles at a crack.

My daily pastimes include attending meetings, sitting through mentoring sessions, and feeding the dogs when Mary's out of town. And finishing this damn book, which has taken much longer than it should.

So, why am I in my bonus years when so many of my childhood friends are not? "Why me?" I whispered to myself as I crawled under the covers that night, savoring my time spent with Tom's son. "How did I get so lucky?"

Don't get me wrong, I don't spend an inordinate amount of time reflecting on my good fortune. And I don't really feel guilty . . . well, most of the time, anyway.

Instead, I do my best to pay back whoever it was that issued me the Pass Go card that I'm enjoying.

The card that only we lucky ones get.

MY WISDOM:

"Science tells us that humans have an innate biological-aging clock and that for some of us it simply ticks longer."

A Letter to My Grandchildren

"Never have children, only grandchildren."
—GORE VIDAL

GRANDPARENTS ARE GOOD FOR THREE THINGS, at least where our grandchildren are concerned. We are good for getting them riled up when we visit, we are good for waving goodbye after we've riled them up, and we are good for offering them free advice, whether they want it or not.

For those of you who also are grandparents, I'm sure you already know how to rile your grandchildren up and then wave goodbye, but here's an example of how to give them free advice, whether they want it or not;

Dear Andrew, Abby, Tucker, Amanda, and Julia:

I had a grandfather, too. Grandpa Joe was his name and he lived on a small farm in Iowa, down by the Missouri border. I didn't know him well, but I can still picture him sitting on the swing on his front porch, thumbs hooked in his suspenders, telling me that "it's a scary world out there, Jimmy boy, I'm glad I'm not growing up in times like these."

And then he'd snap his suspenders, shake his head, and sometimes drift off to sleep.

Fortunately for you, you're not going to hear that kind of negative advice from me. This world isn't that bad a place, if you don't watch the six o'clock news and if you have a grandparent nearby to keep you advised on how the world works and how to make your life worthwhile.

Your mom and dad will have to keep you away from the six o'clock news, but I can help you with the advice part . . .

- *Always adore your grandparents and shower them with love.*
- *Believe in Santa Claus, the tooth fairy, and the innate goodness of your grandparents.*
- *Use all of the crayons, not just the red and blue ones.*
- *Read books. Especially the ones that teach you stuff.*
- *Mow grass, rake leaves, and shovel snow.*
- *Travel; there's a fascinating world out there.*
- *Beware of credit cards, Saturday morning TV, and people who don't look you straight in the eye.*
- *Savor your mother on Mother's Day, your Father on Father's Day, and your grandparents all of the time.*
- *So, there you have it, Andrew, Abby, Tucker, Amanda and Julia. My best advice on how to grow up to be someone your parents and I can be proud of, offered to you on this splendid June day in the year 2005. Call me if you need me and I'll see you for three days sometime before Christmas.*

Love, Grandpa Jim

MY WISDOM:

"When all else fails, ask your grandparents."

PART FOUR

LOOKING BACK

It's OK to look back, I've learned, as long as you don't spend too much time doing it. And as long as you never, ever, stop looking forward. Looking back provides us the opportunity to learn from our mistakes; if you're like me, you've made more than your share of them. Looking back can also open your eyes as to how much your parents and your friends shaped your life. In my case, especially.

Grandson Tuck, Mary, Sister Chris

Grandson Tuck, granddaughter Amanda, and Mary

Mentoring with Maggie

There's a Mom Behind Every Story

"It's too big, this job of being a MOM. I mean, we're still working out our own issues, never mind tackling all the issues our children are dealing with."
—UNKNOWN MOM

MOST OF US AREN'T THINKING ABOUT motherhood when we're watching the carnival that calls itself the 6:00 o'clock news, but behind every story that involves people there's a mom. There was a mother behind John Glenn when he orbited the Earth, there was a mother behind Princess Diana when she lit up the world, and there was a mother behind each of the 911 terrorists, when they turned the world upside down.

And then there was the mom behind the story on Channel 10, San Diego, October 3, 1993. The 6:00 o'clock evening news.

With a set to her jaw, the female TV anchor introduced yet another grisly tale that takes place in a society tinged in violence. The story involved a teenage boy who, for reasons only he and his Maker will ever understand, wrought his frustration by killing four innocent bystanders in a San Diego McDonald's restaurant, then followed by taking his own life.

The anchor grimly but professionally described the incident to her listeners, then switched to an interview with the young man's parents. A warm and expressive couple, I'd welcome them as my neighbor, any time.

I watched as the killer's mother bared her soul for the camera and for those of us on the edge of our chairs. I listened as her heart unleashed a message of sorrow, remorse, and most of all, confusion, over her son's life gone senselessly astray. I ached for her as she concluded the interview with a plea for understanding, a cry for forgiveness, and a call to the society of motherhood.

The anchor, a professional woman if ever there were one, so precise and businesslike over a long and successful career of dispensing news, must have seen and heard it all. But, after the killer's mother had finished speaking, the anchor stared at the camera as if it were a midnight intruder, as if it belonged to the Discovery Channel or ESPN. And then her mouth moved ever so slightly, but nothing came out.

The anchor glanced down at her script, then back to the unforgiving camera again, while Mary and I squirmed in our chairs, waiting and blinking the tears away, sharing her pain. Finally, the anchor's eyes moistened, but they didn't cry.

They bled.

And after what seemed time enough to run a dozen Burger King commercials, she rasped the TV announcer's favorite get-me-out-of-this-jam phrase: "back after this message." Then the screen went dark.

I understood why the anchor's eyes bled. They bled for the mother of the killer, they bled for the mothers of her son's victims, and they bled for the universal society of mothers, herself included. And most of all, the newscaster's eyes bled for the magic of motherhood, however you define it, wherever it takes place.

And my eyes bled too. My eyes bled because the killer's mother could just as well have been my own mom: the similarities between the two women were everywhere. The piercing brown eyes, the pursed lips, the firm set of the jaw. That mom sat ramrod straight in her chair as she was being interviewed, just like my mom used to do when she was straightening me out about something.

My mom was a rock-solid parent and person, and so was the mother of the killer. That was obvious to Mary and I. What happened to her could have happened to any mom, mine included. One horrible decision on the part of her kid would be all that it takes.

It's been twenty-six years since that San Diego TV screen went dark. And I've learned, over those years, that the mother of the killer was as much a victim as the people her son murdered that day.

The crime was not of her doing; her son had grown and flown, and her influence had long ago waned.

But it was she who was left to explain.

MY WISDOM:

"A mom's day-to-day involvement may end but her

responsibility lasts forever."

The Day Our Country Didn't Feel Safe Anymore

"The world may never be normal again. But this is my life now. I have to live it." —MANU DHINGRA

THERE ARE ONLY A FEW LIFE-CHANGING events where we can remember exactly where we were and what we were doing when we heard the news. For me, the assassination of President Kennedy (I was at work) was one; man's landing on the moon was another (a Lake Michigan vacation); and, of course, the 21st century's version of the Day of Infamy, September 11, 2001.

Every American has their own, heart-rending story of that tragic day. Ours began in the late afternoon of September 10 when Mary concluded a sales call in Waterloo, Iowa. The following morning, she rose early to catch a commuter flight from Waterloo to Minneapolis, in what was supposed to be the beginning of a day of travel that would deliver her to Bend by nightfall.

Her first leg completed, she was perched comfortably in the Northwest Airlines World Club in Minneapolis when the first plane slammed into the South Tower of the World Trade Center. Rising voices attracted her to an ashen group of travelers huddled around an overhead TV. Horrified, she watched as one of the world's most identifiable landmarks erupted into a giant torch.

Aghast, she called me at home. It was a few minutes before 7:00 a.m. in Bend. I was dawdling in bed, digesting the morning newspaper—my way of misbehaving when she's out of town.

"Quick, turn on the TV," she said sharply, without a greeting. "You won't believe what you see."

I flicked on the bedroom TV and was instantly shaken by the sight that we Americans will remember for the rest of our lives. The South Tower was a volcano of fire and smoke.

"I'm frightened," she whispered uncharacteristically, her voice quavering. "I want to come home."

I tried to calm her and seconds later she was back in control. It was time to head to the gate for her flight to Portland, on the way back to Bend. I wished her safe travels and remained glued to the TV.

Suddenly, a second plane banked into the screen and, as I screamed a senseless warning, buried its nose in the North Tower.

Flames now spiraled from both towers, and the TV pundits babbled incoherently as their equally incoherent audience stared in disbelief. Perhaps we were watching some sort of a latter-day George Orwell stunt or the latest release of a Hollywood action film spliced into the major TV channels.

My phone rang again.

"You saw the second plane?" Mary gushed breathlessly, more statement than question.

"I did."

"They've cancelled all the flights out of Minneapolis," she continued. "People are scared, they're running down the corridors. It's not chaos, but it's close."

"I'm going to try and rent a car," she was shouting now, trying to be heard above the background din. "I can stay in Minneapolis with my brother until things settle down. It'll take at least ten minutes to get to the Avis counter. I won't be the only one heading there, so please call Avis and see if you can get a confirmation number. I'll call you back as soon as I reach the counter."

I ran downstairs to my office and dialed Avis, at the same time logging on to the Internet. No surprise, the 800 line was busy. I tried again. Still no luck.

I punched redial on the phone, then asked Google to take me to the Avis website. A couple of keystrokes later and I pulled up a reservation form. Another minute or so of typing and I had a hallowed confirmation number in my hand. Technology couldn't care less what kind of hell the world is going through, which is one of the reasons why it will never fully replace us.

My phone rang again. "I'm standing in the Avis line." She was breathing hard, no doubt from outsprinting a pack of men to capture her place in line. "The line's a mile long. Any luck?"

I gave her the hallowed confirmation number and we exchanged a quick goodbye. I later learned that several minutes following our conversation, a harried Avis agent had announced to the waiting crowd that anyone without a confirmation number would not get a car.

Mary got hers.

For the next five days she holed up with her brother Jerry in suburban Minneapolis. Patience not being her strong suit, she could only let the situation control her for so long. Finally, she talked Jerry into driving her to Billings, Montana, an 800-mile drive west and one-half of the distance between Minneapolis and Bend. I made a similar 800-mile drive east, we connected, and were on the road back to Bend the following morning.

The Cascade Mountains were framed by the setting sun as we pulled into our driveway following the twelve-hour drive home. We stepped out of the car, took a deep breath of Bend's sweet air and looked west as the sun dipped slowly behind the mountains.

Neither of us spoke. There was no need to.

MY WISDOM:

"The world will change. But what won't change is home. It will always be there when we need it."

The Best Place to Find Heroes

"Those who say that we're in a time when there are no heroes, they just don't know where to look."
—RONALD REAGAN, FIRST INAUGURAL
ADDRESS, JAN. 20, 1981

IT ALL STARTED WITH A QUESTION over a beer. I asked my friend Peter who his heroes were when he was growing up.

"Well," he said with a grin, no doubt recalling fond memories, "I'd have to say Y. A. Tittle (a football icon), Bob Lee (a role model), and Andy Mershon (a mentor)." We discussed his choices and how they impacted his life.

"And yours?" Peter asked in return.

"Oh, I had a million of 'em," I replied. Most were athletes, because that's all I knew when I was a kid.

"I'd say my top three were Stan Musial, Ben Hogan, and, of course, the Yankees' good old number seven, Mickey Mantle."

We laughed at the mention of The Mick. A hero on the field, we've since learned he was anything but in his personal life.

"How about today?" I persisted. "Who are your heroes on the national stage right now?"

"Whew, that's a tough one," Peter said, following a long silence. "It's hard to come up with more than a couple." We spent an hour debating a miniscule list of modern-day heroes that lived up to our standards.

Dictionary.com tells its readers that *"a hero is someone who, in the opinion of others, has special achievements, abilities, or personal qualities and is regarded as a role model or ideal."* Lots of people, we agreed, would qualify as heroes based on their achievements or abilities; the hard part is living up to the "role model or ideal" phrase.

That discussion marked the beginning of our annual Hero Identification contest. Fifteen years later it continues, sans the beer; Peter now lives in Portland and I live in in Bend. A couple of times every year we'll update the list via phone or email.

"Any deletions or additions?" I'll ask.

"Take Tiger off the list," he'll reply. Or "Add Condoleezza Rice."

"And John Glenn?"

"He stays," says Peter, who leans to the left. "Politics aside, he's earned his star."

And then I give Peter my additions and deletions and the longer we do this, the more depressed we become. Old fashioned heroes, on the national stage anyway, the kind that make us feel like our world is in good hands, are difficult to come by.

Before the days of Google, it took years of history to uncover who the heroes were and weren't. JFK was a hero when I was in my twenties, same as The Mick when I was ten. Yet neither make the list today, JFK had too many dicey escapades on his resume and The Mick had too many ribald biographies written about him. Sooner or later, time and truth catches up with us all.

Sadly, there are plenty of heroes on the national scene, but the problem is we don't hear about them. They are our soldiers, scientists, doctors, educators, entrepreneurs, and other little-known but contributing citizens—people who have left their mark on the world but won't be appearing on the 6 o'clock news. We don't hear about them because the good things people do don't sell papers or attract TV viewers. It's the tawdry stuff that sucks up the media's attention.

This hero exercise led Peter and me to introduce a twist to our rating game. Instead of limiting our hero search to the national or worldwide stage, we brought it down to the local level. To the communities we live in. To Portland and Bend.

The results were telling. In Bend, population 100,000, I can rattle off a dozen local heroes in the time it takes to tie my shoes. Give me a bit more time and I'll double that number. Peter can do the same for Portland, and I'll bet you could for your community, too.

MY WISDOM:

"Any time you're looking for a hero, no need to

look any further. You can find all you want

right at home."

The Power of a Third Dimension

*"Do not follow where the path may lead. Go instead
where there is no path and leave a trail."*
—RALPH WALDO EMERSON

"JIM," MY FRIEND JEN SAID, HER eyes on fire, "You'll love this
story; it's about a life-changing experience I'm about to have." She
set her coffee down and leaned forward in her chair, elbows on the
table.

"I'm leaving for Barcelona in two weeks," she continued. "I'll be
joined by 143 other people from around the world. 143 people like
me, people who want to do something to make our world a better
place to live."

"We can't just stand by and watch things continue to fall apart,"
she went on. "One hundred and forty-four of us are determined to
help turn things around, to try and make a better world. Or at least,"
she concluded, "we're gonna try."

"Sounds fascinating," I replied. "But 144 people? Change the
world? Sounds like a tall order to me."

"We're part of an organization called Le Ciel," she continued
unabated. "Le Ciel is French for The Sky, which is what we'll be
reaching for."

"That's nothing new for you," I replied with a smile.

"OK, I know," she said, rolling her eyes. "But this time I'm not alone. I'll be part of a team, an organized team, and we're committed to moving the needle."

She went on to explain that Le Ciel is a UK-based foundation whose mission is to restore harmony and ecology on a global scale through cultural, spiritual and environmental projects. To achieve their lofty goals, in early December 2018, Le Ciel assembled 144 talented and motivated people from around the world (the only criterion being that each person must speak English), divided them into twelve teams of twelve people each, and sent them off on a year-long search for harmony and ecology-based solutions. Then, one year after that first meeting, the teams would reconvene and report on what they've learned and what they've accomplished, to an auditorium filled with peers, foundations, and potential investors.

"And then," she continued, "who knows? Maybe the money will follow, and the project will get funded and carried forward. Odds are that some of the twelve teams are going to make something real and tangible happen."

"Jen," I said when she paused, "while Le Ciel sounds a tad woo-woo to my skeptical mind, I know that won't slow you down. Nor should it. I agree that, from what you've told me and the passion with which you've expressed it, this could be a life-changing opportunity for you. It sounds like you'll be adding a brand, new dimension to your life. A third dimension."

A "third dimension" is, by my definition anyway, that additional dimension – supplementing the family and work ones—that some people need in order to make them feel whole and complete. It's that dimension that—when the work and family day is done—fills our mind and invades our dreams and becomes the first thing we think about when our eyes flutter open in the morning.

The pursuit of a Third Dimension is about being fulfilled and satisfying one's soul through service to others. It could be found on a global scale or we can find it right at home. The key is committing to a cause, be it Le Ciel, our local boys and girls club, or our community's family kitchen.

While I admire Le Ciel's global mission, it's too broad a vision for me, too gray, too abstract, too difficult to envisage. The gratification period is also too long, I like those projects where I can see measurable results today, tomorrow, or next week.

But having a Third Dimension in life makes plenty of sense to me. It will never replace family and work, but it can add variety and sense of mission in a world that needs all the help it can get.

MY WISDOM:

"Two dimensions are a blessing. A third dimension

is a bonus."

Millennials Get a Bad Rap. Well, Sorta . . .

The Millennial's Mantra: "Don't lament so much about how your career is going to turn out. You don't have a career. You have a life. —ADUNOLA ADESHOLA

SEVERAL YEARS AGO, MY FRIEND PETER and I decided to take a late-winter golf jaunt to San Diego, the land of afternoon sun, salty air, and clogged highways. We chose the Torrey Pines Golf Course as our destination. Torrey, as it is known to the golf community, is San Diego's iconic, eucalyptus-lined, public-course-gone-upscale, resting regally atop towering cliffs that overlook the Pacific Ocean. Torrey hosts an official PGA golf tournament every year, which makes it a tourist attraction for golfaholic people like us.

Torrey is also a *public* golf course, which means that it welcomes anyone with a credit card and a set of golf clubs. As a result, it's a melting pot for amateur hackers like Peter and myself, people who want to enjoy the same golf course that Tiger Woods plays.

We were paired that day with Brad and Andy, two mellow Millennials from San Diego. Like us, they too felt fortunate to be enjoying a fine golf course on a sunlit day, a weekday when the rest of the world was busy solving its problems. Brad and Andy's golfing talent levels were no threat to the reigning PGA tour professionals (ditto for Peter and me), which means we all could shrug and shake it off when our golf ball spiraled off in directions it wasn't supposed to go.

As the round progressed and the pace of play slowed, I started asking questions of our two playing partners. After all, two relaxed Millennials didn't cross my path every day, I couldn't resist the opportunity.

"So, tell me Brad," I inquired of the taller one with bulging muscles and a dragon tattoo on his left forearm. "What's your role in life?" (One of my favorite questions because you're never quite sure what's coming next).

"I'm a mason," Brad replied simply, a touch of pride in his voice.

"That's cool," I replied, and it did sound cool, especially to someone like me who can't change a lightbulb by myself.

"And how about you, Andy?" I asked of Brad's sandy-haired companion.

"Goin' to Cabo," Andy replied, in the same tone of voice he'd use to order a quarter pounder with cheese.

Say what, Andy? How can your role in life be "goin' to Cabo?" OK, so I know that Cabo San Lucas is a favorite destination for thousands of the West Coast's young and restless, but is going there your role in life? I mean, goin' to Cabo? Now really, Andy, isn't that setting your expectations a bit low?

Could it be that my expectations were misaligned? I wondered. The more I thought about Goin to Cabo, the more I couldn't wrap my arms around that being a role in someone's life. OK, so I *could* understand Goin' to Cabo for what it is—a jaunt, a party, a break in the action. A long weekend of socializing, sunning, and draining one's checkbook. I get that.

But I wanted to say to Andy that Goin' to Cabo can't be the first and foremost reason why, at this point in time, you're here on this earth. When I was his age (oh, oh, here I go again), my role in life was to feed five hungry faces while holding down a job I didn't like. If I was goin' anywhere, it would have been to Whitey's Ice Cream store on a Saturday afternoon with my kids.

But Andy's response, sounded so, well, so shortsighted, so today, so this minute, so right now.

Yet, today, a dozen years since and a lot of Millennial-experiences later, I now understand Andy's response. I'm sure Andy had had a job of some sort at the time, maybe even one that was fulfilling for him. But he needed a break because, unlike my generation, he and his Millennial friends have a different outlook on life. They have chosen to work to live rather than live to work, as my generation did.

Whether we oldtimers are fans of Andy's Goin' to Cabo philosophy or not, he's going to enjoy himself every chance he gets.

He'll worry about his role in life when he's back in town.

MY WISDOM:

"No need to worry about the next generation not

'getting it.' The generation previous to yours said

the same thing about you."

Technology: It's Good for the World, but Baffling to Me

"The internet is the single most important development in the history of human communication since the invention of call waiting." —DAVE BARRY

I'M CONSTANTLY AMAZED AT THE CREATIVE and unthinkable things that technology can do. Alexa can answer our questions, tell us jokes, or sell us a pool table in less time than it takes to butter a piece of toast. Technology can also remember a spouse's birthday (whatever happened to Post-Its on our refrigerator door?), vacuum the living room floor, or scoop up the dog's poop while its owner takes a nap.

I enjoy reading about the latest pocket-sized mobile miracle or the latest new app that does things most of us never realized we'd need done. I'm flabbergasted at what those little chips, sensors, and bots can do to make our life easier, whether we want it made easier or not.

But, as with everything else, there are downsides. Here's a personal story that's painful to tell but reflects exactly what I'm talking about.

———

It's a crisp fall day in October of 2016. I needed to print the calendar I keep on my iPad, in case the IRS asked for proof of my mileage deduction. Having no clue how to pull off such a trick, I took the problem to Suzanne, the President of Mary's company and someone who is genetically enhanced to deal with such things. Mary joined us in Suzanne's office, since she is our family's resident geek and is often entertained by my technology shortcomings.

Suzanne opened the calendar on my iPad, then asked to see my iPhone. (I knew better than to ask why). She then turned to her desktop and pulled up instructions on what to do from a website I've never heard of.

"It'll cost you $2 to print your calendar," she said, looking up from the screen.

"Who gets the $2?" I replied, forever wondering about such things.

"It doesn't matter, Jim" Mary chimed in, shaking her head. She'd heard my irrelevant questions before.

"What's your Apple ID password?" Suzanne asked.

I looked up my password on a folded piece of 8 ½ x 11 paper I carry with me wherever I go. The sheet is scribbled on both sides, I have more passwords than socks.

Suzanne entered the password I gave her. "Sorry, doesn't work," she reported, in a tone of voice that said she wasn't the least bit surprised.

"I have his passwords on my iPad," Mary added. Click, click her fingers flew. She gave Suzanne a password. It worked.

"I need your Visa card number now," Suzanne went on, undeterred.

This much I could handle.

Click, click Suzanne's fingers went, quickly followed by "Oops, your Visa card has expired. What's your new number?"

"I have it right here" Mary replied, saving me from shrugging my shoulders.

All I wanted to do was print a couple of lousy calendars. My head began to throb, I knew I should be keeping my calendars on paper.

Suzanne received clearance from the website's mission control and resumed her pecking, while Mary looked on over her shoulder. Meanwhile, I studied my shoes, which could use a shine.

Suzanne then showed us – well, she showed Mary – several more iPad-related tasks that needed completing before the printer could do its work. Click, click, click, her keyboard sang. How do people remember all those different commands that get you to this point?

Twenty minutes after I'd walked into Suzanne's office, I slunk out, printed calendars in hand. But that wasn't all I walked out with. My head was throbbing now.

Next stop, the cleaners.

"Hi Jim," sang Abby, the smiling Millennial behind the counter. "How are you today?"

"Fried," I grumbled.

"I'm sorry," she answered, "your eyes do look kinda glassy."

I began to explain what I'd just been through, but it made my headache worse, so I quit.

"Man, do I hate technology," I concluded. Abby smiled, then handed me a digital device that needed my electronic signature. I signed it in the wrong place.

"I know what you mean about technology," she said, thumbing her iPhone without looking up. "My daughter's struggling with it too, but then, so's most of her kindergarten class."

MY WISDOM:

"Don't fight it, the only way to solve your

technology problems is to have a friendly geek

on speed dial."

Find a Career You Can Love

"Find a job you love, and you'll never work another day in your life." — CONFUCIUS

REMEMBER MY EARLIER STORY ABOUT TIM, the boy on my hockey team who lost his dad in the middle of the season? I was thirty-two at the time I was coaching that team; I had a wife, three hungry sons, and a career that was going nowhere. I also had a job I didn't love, lived in a neighborhood I couldn't afford, and was working for my third employer since graduating from college. To make matters worse, those were the days of the single household income, when one partner (in our case, my wife) stayed at home to raise the kids. Which meant that I was *it* where our family's financial well-being was concerned.

We were paying the bills, but just barely.

While struggling through those times, thanks to those three going-nowhere jobs, I also discovered that having a job that pays the bills isn't enough. What I needed was a job that paid the bills AND stirred my soul, which, in turn, would motivate me to care about what I was doing. In short, I needed a job I could love.

Shortly after Tim's hockey season ended, I decided it was time to make the big change. To roll the dice on my life. My role as working for someone else wasn't the answer: I'd had a procession of bosses, none of whom inspired me, and vice versa, I'm sure. My life was stuck in neutral. No, make that in reverse.

The number one thing that needed to change? The person I worked for. I'd learned the hard way that working for someone else wouldn't hack it.

I needed to work for me. I needed to be my own boss.

I needed to own a small business.

Today, we call people who own small businesses "entrepreneurs." That word wasn't part of the business lexicon in the 1960s, and those of us who owned a small business were called just that: "small business owners." Or in some cases a "mom and pop" business owner. Not nearly as sexy as being an "entrepreneur," but the career was the same.

The decision to become a small business owner changed my viewpoint on what work was all about. Instead of collecting a paycheck signed by someone else, I now signed my paycheck myself, along with the paychecks of all the other folks who were working for me. Yes, I'd opted for freedom, but as is always the case, freedom comes with a price. That price is responsibility, which means I was now responsible not only for me, but also for all my employees.

As it turned out, nine years after finishing college, with three unsatisfying jobs under my belt, I finally found what I was looking for—a career I could love. In 1970 I bought a small sporting goods business, one that was languishing in bankruptcy when I stumbled on it.

And with *that* . . . drum roll please . . . I officially became a small business owner. An entrepreneur.

At age 32, I'd finally found a career I could love.

A recent Gallup poll discovered that 70 percent of today's Americans are "disengaged from their jobs." How sad is that, it's hard to comprehend someone spending the roughly 80,000 hours he or she will be working over a forty-year career in a "disengaged" state. Heck, I spend my first 18,000 in that state myself, which was more than enough. There aren't *that* many hours in our life as it is, wasting 18,000 of them is not a sound strategy.

All five of my grandkids are Millennials. My wish for them is that they spend as few of their 80,000 working hours being "disengaged" as possible. Go ahead, I've advised them (whether they wanted to be advised or not), job-hop 'til you find a job you can love. Try twenty different jobs if that's what it takes, but don't dawdle. The fewer of those 80,000 hours you waste finding a job you can love, the better.

My hope for them is that they, like me, will become passionate and energized by the work that they do. I want them to leap out of bed in the morning, whistle while they shower, and bounce off the walls once they get to their office.

Work can be fun. When, that is, your work is meaningful to you.

MY WISDOM:

"It's better to have a dozen jobs and find the right

fit, then to have one job and never find the right

fit at all."

The Lessons I Learned from My Mom

"Eat your carrots, they're good for your eyes," my mom used to tell me. But I hated carrots, so I'd do everything I could to avoid them. Today I'm blind in one eye. Who says that moms don't know what's best for us?"
—JIM SCHELL

I WAS HAVING LUNCH WITH JULIE, a recently retired friend, when she pulled out a pencil and notebook. I'd been her friend and mentor over the past fifteen years of her working career, but assumed those mentoring days were over.

"Oh-oh," I said, as she thumbed through the notebook looking for a fresh page. "You're taking notes? What's going on here? Are you going back to work?"

"Well, yes, I kinda am, depending on how you define work," she replied, her fork toying with her salad. "Jim, are you ready for this? I'm going to be, for the next year anyway . . . a baby-sitter."

"Now that's a career change," I replied with a chuckle. She'd been one of Bend's leading bankers for years.

"Oh, I'm not going to babysit for just any baby," she laughed. Then a smile wider than her salad plate crossed her face. "I'm going to be a grandmother!"

"Hey, congratulations!" I replied, raising my Pepsi in a toast. We clinked glasses.

"But you'll be babysitting? Every day? Come rain or shine?" She'd recently retired and had been, up to now, basking in her new-found freedom.

"I'd rather babysit for my grandchild than anything else I can think of right now," she replied, her mouth firm. "Why wouldn't I want to do the most important thing a person can do?"

"And that is?" I replied, setting myself up.

"Raise a child," she replied, in the tone of voice that people use when answering stupid questions.

"Yes, but . . . " I began.

"No yes-buts about it, Jim. A person's life begins under the influence of his or her parents. I want to be part of that influence. Better me than a daycare provider."

And then my light went on. She'd frequently mentioned reinventing the role of grandmotherhood as her banking career was winding down. This upcoming grandkid didn't know it yet, but he or she was about to become the highlight of a grandmother's life.

"Well, I'm happy for you," I continued. "But you're not expecting help from me on babysitting, are you? I haven't changed a diaper in years."

"Oh, I've got the diaper thing covered," she said, rolling her eyes. "No, I want to be the world's greatest grandmother ever, so I'm looking for help from my friends. In that vein, I have a question for you."

"Fire away," I replied, expectantly. She always asked good questions.

"You've spoken frequently about how much your mom influenced your life. What exactly did she do for you? What made her so good? What can I learn from her?"

See what I mean about good questions.

So, with the admission that I was a long way from being the perfect kid, and that I come up a tad lacking in the adult category too, here's how, over a lunch of fish and chips, I answered Julie's question . . .

Important Lessons My Mom Taught Me

- Be punctual. Five o'clock means five o'clock, not five minutes after five.
- Keep your mind active. When a member of her bridge club couldn't make it, I was the fill-in.
- Read books. She was a member of the Book-of-the-Month Club and kept me up to speed on everything she deemed worth reading.
- Ask questions. "Interested is interesting" was her favorite adage, and she never let me forget what it meant.
- Listen to learn. She was an early adopter when it came to "listening to learn, not to respond."
- Mind your grammar. Ending a sentence in a preposition was something up with which she would not put.
- And finally, drum roll please, I learned from my mom that we are accountable for our actions. When I trashed my freshman year in college at Boulder, I spent my sophomore year in Des Moines.

I was eons away from being the perfect kid growing up, and maybe Mom wasn't the perfect mom either, but she was close. We each had our shortcomings, yet together we grew this imperfect son into a contributing adult, and for that I will be forever grateful.

I wish Mom could come back, just for a day. We could have lunch; I'd suggest she order the fish and chips at the restaurant that Julie and I visited. The batter was light, and the chips fresh and crunchy.

First, I'd say thanks, Mom, for staying with me when I took the wrong path. Then I'd compliment her for her tough love on those all-too-frequent occasions when I let her down.

And finally, I'd apologize for that freshman year in college. I'll bet she's still shaking her head over that.

MY WISDOM:

"Dads make the family, but moms make the child."

Interested Is Interesting

"You can tell whether a man is clever by his answers.
You can tell whether a man is wise by his questions."
—NAGUIB MAHFOUZ, NOBEL PRIZE WINNER

YOU TURN THE CORNER AND HERE comes Bill, a longtime friend, walking towards you. You haven't seen him for months.

"Hey, Bill, long time no see," you say. "How ya doin?"

"Pretty good, Jim. How ya doin'?"

"I'm doin' pretty good, too."

Wow, now who wouldn't want to party with these two guys? What a stimulating night of conversation that would be.

Let's take a different tack in looking at the above conversation. What if we changed the dialogue to . . .

"Hi, Bill, long time no see," you say. "On a scale of one to ten, how's your life these days?"

"Scale of one to ten?" Bill replies, scratching his head. "Well, gee Jim, I dunno. I guess maybe a . . . a six."

"A six?" you reply, your warning light switching on. "What would it take to get it to an eight?"

And then Bill tells you why his life is a six. And maybe you can help him get it to an eight and maybe you can't. But if you don't ask, you'll never have the chance.

Or, on the flip side, if Bill's life is a nine or ten, wouldn't you want to know that too?

I can blame my mom for getting me on this question-asking kick. Good questions, she would tell Chris and me, are always more difficult to come up with than good answers.

When Chris and I were kids, Mom's questions would rain down on us like confetti on a Thanksgiving Day parade. Early on, they were the growing-up kind of questions that moms like to ask, such as "where do you think rain comes from," or "why do you think the sky is blue," or "what kind of cookies should we leave for Santa?"

Later on, while I was living at home during the summer of my sophomore year in college, her questions took on a more information-gathering tone such as "why did you get home at 2 a.m. last night?" or "who were you with when you didn't get home until 2 a.m. last night?" or "why are your eyes so red?"

"You can't learn anything when your mouth is moving," Mom would scold, and the years have proven her right.

Today I carry on her tradition of asking questions at the drop of a hat, to the consternation of some of my friends. "Please, let's not invite Jim to our dinner party," I'm sure has been said more times than I need to know. "He asks too many questions."

Sometimes I worry about my reputation as the Question Man. To those who've expressed concern over this habit of mine, I've apologized profusely on more than one occasion, assuring them I'm not trying to piss them off. I can't help it, I explain, my mother passed on her question-asking DNA to me.

I don't tell my naysayers this, but my mom's DNA is not the only reason I ask questions. I've learned over the years that by asking questions, I don't have to listen to my friend's tell me about their cat, their summer vacation, or last month's hernia operation.

If you, like me, believe in the power of asking questions, here are several examples of how to elicit interesting answers to those traditional questions that too often result in boring answers. Answers like "OK" or "pretty good" or "cool."

Instead of: "How was school today?" followed by your kid responding "OK." You ask: "What's the number one thing you learned in school today?"

Instead of: "How was your vacation?" followed by your friend responding, "pretty good." You ask: "What was the favorite thing you did on your vacation?"

Instead of: "How was Disneyland?" followed by your next-door neighbor responding "cool." You ask: "What was the favorite thing you did at Disneyland?"

In case you're wondering, my number one, all-time favorite question is: *"if this were a perfect world, what will you be doing five years from now?"* Of course, the time, place, and askee need to be right for that question, but when they are, hold on to your hat—all kinds of unexpected responses can result. Waiters, bartenders, folks who are about to retire, and recent college graduates are among my favorite targets for this question. If you're one of those people and I see you on the street, don't say I didn't warn you.

Getting back to Mom and her role in this question-asking addiction of mine: "interested is interesting" was her favorite adage and provided the basis for her love of asking questions. "If someone I meet is interested in talking about something other than themselves, I'll be interested in them," she'd tell Chris and me, explaining how the adage works.

On the flip side, if someone starts a conversation by talking about themselves, Mom would make a beeline for the exit.

Start that conversation by asking a question, however, and she'd have a new friend.

MY WISDOM:

"Questions open the door to collecting wisdom,

talking closes the door."

The Power of Passion

"In a world too full of people who couldn't care less, be someone who couldn't care more." —ANONYMOUS

DESPITE MY MISGIVINGS ABOUT TELEVISION, I'VE been known to watch a reality show called *Shark Tank*. In that show, prospective entrepreneurs who want to start their own business make their pitch to five professional investors – the Sharks. If the Sharks like what they hear, they make an offer to invest in the entrepreneur's business, thereby providing him or her with much-needed cash. If they don't like what they hear, they send the deflated soul back to his or her day job.

In one 2013 episode, Mary and I watched as a woman with a dazzling smile pitched her business idea to the five Sharks (four men and one woman). Following her presentation and a lengthy Q&A session, each Shark took their turn giving the woman a variety of reasons why they were turning thumbs down on investing in her business. (Note to ABC: The male Sharks, two of them especially, could use some sensitivity training).

After the final Shark had rendered his rejection, the camera zoomed in on the woman. She continued to stand on the stage, motionless, her face frozen, her eyes downcast, for what seemed like an eternity. Even the jaded Sharks studied their shoes and checked their fingernails, doing everything they could to avoid looking at this woman whose dreams had just been dashed in front of millions of viewers. Meanwhile, her face turned a pasty white and her dazzling smile turned upside down.

Upon being rejected, the presenter is supposed to exit stage left. But the woman remained in a trance, frozen where she stood, while a cascade of tears ran down her cheeks and splashed on the stage floor. Then her hands turned palms up as if pleading for understanding from someone – we viewers, perhaps? Didn't we know how hard she had worked, how successful her business would be, how much she cared?

Time and the program stood still.

Suddenly, the lone female Shark (Lori, for those of you who watch the show), spoke up. "I reverse my decision," she said. "I'll give you $65,000 in exchange for 25% equity in your business." Was that a glistening of moisture I spotted in Lori's eyes?

The woman's tears stopped and her smile returned, brighter and wider than before. Then she lunged forward to meet the oncoming Lori and the two women embraced in an emotional hug.

Well, maybe the woman's tears disappeared, but Mary's didn't and neither did mine. And I'll bet they didn't for millions of other viewers too: the scene was as touching and emotional as reality TV can get.

Lori, as she admitted after the woman had danced off the set, did not invest in her business because the idea was so compelling or the presentation so stellar. Rather, she invested because she could feel the depth of the presenter's passion—for her business and for her product. She could see and feel how much the woman cared.

"It's no coincidence that it took an empathetic woman to reverse her decision, while the four men looked on like dogs watching a cat eat their dinner," Mary sniffed, wiping her eyes.

Passion prevails, I was once again reassured by that television show. It's that way in business and it's that way in life.

MY WISDOM:

"It isn't the idea that makes the difference, it's the passion of the person behind the idea."

Paying It Forward

"It is one of the beautiful compensations in this life that no one can sincerely try to help another without helping himself." —RALPH WALDO EMERSON.

ON A COOL DECEMBER EVENING IN Tucson, Mary and I had dinner with Gretchen and Sue, good friends and golfing buddies. They're generous donors to a string of Tucson nonprofits, but this year, in addition to writing checks, they'd decided to add a new dimension to their holiday giving. As they explained to us over a dinner of my world-famous beef stroganoff, they decided to do something more than write a check.

They decided to do something they could see, touch, and most of all, feel.

So, on a sunny afternoon a week or so later, Gretchen and Sue went shopping at Walmart. Not for something they needed, but for someone they could help. Their intention? To pick up the tab for a yet-to-be-identified Christmas shopper. Someone who, in their view, needed help picking up the tab.

Following an hour of eavesdropping and peering around corners, the ladies finally found the shopper they were searching for. Obviously a young mother, the woman looked as if she were someone who could use, and would appreciate, an unexpected gift. She was slowly pushing her cart through the toy department, carefully checking off her selections against a shopping list. From there, she moved on to the clothing department, with Gretchen and Sue spying on her from behind the jacket rack.

Finally, her shopping list complete, the woman approached the cashier line.

"Excuse me," Gretchen said, putting her hand on the woman's shoulder as she was about to unload her cart, "may we please pay for your purchases?"

"I . . . I . . . don't understand" the woman stammered, her brow furrowed.

"We want to give you a Christmas present. We'd like to pay for what's in your cart," Sue answered, her eyes moist.

Suddenly, the woman realized what was happening and began to cry. Not to be outdone, so did Gretchen and Sue. And then, right there, before God and dozens of Walmart shoppers, the three women engaged in a laughing, crying, Christmas hug-fest.

Three women in a huddle, crying and hugging, cannot go unnoticed. The cashier, realizing what was going on, hurried around the counter and joined in. So did the shopper next in line.

"You know," Sue said afterwards, as she was telling the story, "in addition to being heartwarming, that experience gave us a reminder of what Christmas is supposed to be about."

As a result of Gretchen and Sue's story, Mary and I decided to test the theory ourselves. We followed their example and, sure enough, we too learned that face-to-face giving beats the heck out of writing a check. And we too went home with a renewed outlook on the true meaning behind the frenzy that is known as Christmas.

The morning following our Walmart experience, we ran out of milk, prompting my trip to the neighborhood convenience store. Milk in hand, I was approaching the cashier, when a Hispanic man, maybe half my age, smiled at me and pulled out his wallet.

"May I pay for your purchase, senor?" he asked.

Startled, I asked him why he was doing this, to which he replied with a smile "it makes me feel good."

I swear, never in my eighty years, not once, had anything like this ever happened to me. And here it was, the day following our Walmart excursion.

Was it serendipity at work? Or was it ordained?

Or, more likely, was it paying it forward, keeping the chain moving?

The day following the milk experience, I stopped in the same convenience store for a soda. The cashier was the same woman who'd been on duty the previous day, so I asked her for the back-story on the man who paid for my milk. "He just likes to do things for people. He does this kind of stuff all the time," she told me. "I have another woman who comes in every week or so and gives me twenty dollars for the next four coffee drinker's purchases.

"I see a lot of this kind of thing," she concluded with a smile that said she knew exactly why "this kind of thing" happens.

I tipped the convenience store cashier as I left, something I've never done before. I didn't plan to do it, I didn't think about doing it, I just did it. It was a reflex action, I suppose, like what you do when someone smiles at you. You smile back.

Returning home, I told Mary about the cashier's comments and about my reaction. "I've never done that before," I added.

"That's funny," she replied with a smile. "I tipped the garbage collector this morning. First time ever for that."

MY WISDOM:

"Paying It Forward is the best way I know to

Pay It Back."

Learning from Our Failures

"I have not failed. I've just found 10,000 ways that won't work." —THOMAS A. EDISON

WE'VE ALL WRITTEN A RESUME AT one time or another, right? Or a curriculum vitae, or CV, or bio, or some sort of document designed to interest someone in us, usually a prospective employer. A resume is, in effect, a historical compilation of our successes; a record showing what an accomplished businessman or woman we've become and/or how cool a person we are.

"Wow," we want the reader to say, "I want to hire this person." Or "I want to get to know her." Or "I want to be her friend."

The resume is, in effect, a sales or connection document and is designed solely for the benefit of the person reading it. But, while the reader is going to learn something from reading it, what will we learn from preparing it? Not much, I'm sorry to say, at least in the typical sense of preparing a resume.

But wait, what if, instead of writing a compilation of our successes, we would write one of our failures? Call it a Failure Resume. It would be a record of our mistakes, our struggles, and our failures along the way. The stuff we've done in life that makes us wish we could have a do-over.

Why would we want to do anything so preposterous? Who would benefit from a review of our biggest failures?

We would, that's who. Because, as Barry Manilow sings in his hit song God Bless the Other 99:

I learned more from failure than I learned from success
I learned from no thank you, so much more than from yes
I learned to be willing to lead with my chin
And if I were willing to lose, I could win

To give you a sense of how a Failure Resume would look, here's a short version of my own. (Shhh, don't tell anyone. This is just between the two of us).

First Marriage

- Failure: Ended after twenty-six years.
- Reason: Married the wrong person. (She did too.)
- Lesson: Involve the head as well as the heart when making life-changing decisions.

Freshman Year in College

- Failure: A 1.56 GPA.
- Reason: Immaturity.
- Lesson: Accountability: To myself and to my parents.

Career Search

- Failure: Took ten years following college graduation to find a career I could love.
- Reason: Stayed too long in jobs I didn't like, even though I knew they were wrong after three months.
- Lesson: When something isn't working, cut your losses and move on.

Biggest Entrepreneurial Venture
(Using someone else's money)
- Failure: Built an ice arena. Came in way over budget.
- Reason: Knew nothing about construction.
- Lesson: Know thyself, especially thy weaknesses.

Biggest Entrepreneurial Venture
(Using my own money)

- Failure: Had to sell my fourth and most successful business before its time.
- Reason: Me? Good entrepreneur, but lousy manager. That business had 200 employees, which was out of my comfort zone.
- Lesson: Know thyself (again). Don't try to do something you can't do. Don't try to be someone you aren't.

My Mom
- Failure: Didn't realize how much she had done for me until after she was gone.
- Reason: Too busy growing up, raising a family, pursuing a career.
- Lesson: Step back. Take an inventory. Don't take meaningful relationships for granted.

These are, incidentally, just the 30,000-foot failures I've made over 83 years of failing. If I were to whittle that altitude down to, say, 1,000 feet and include such failures as the schools I didn't get accepted by, the wrong people I hired, and the people that have taken advantage of my trust in them, the list would be too long for this book.

There's plenty of ways to learn the important lessons in life, but failure is the most impactful teacher of them all. Heck, most of us will forget much of the good stuff we read or are taught, but there's no way we'll forget the bad stuff; the stuff that costs us money, time, and esteem. These are the kind of lessons that last forever.

MY WISDOM:

"Failing is part of life's path that leads to

succeeding."

When It's Time to Retire, Please Consider This

"When I stand before God at the end of my life, I would hope that I would have not a single bit of talent left and could say "I used everything you gave me."
—ERMA BOMBECK

THE KAUFFMAN FOUNDATION RECENTLY ANNOUNCED THAT more Boomers than Millennials are starting businesses these days. So, what's up with that statistic I wondered? Heck, when my dad turned 60, he was counting the days 'til he could sleep in in the morning. Continuing to work was not on his radar. Ditto with a lot of people I know.

Me at that same age? I was trying to figure out what I wanted to do next, but, I knew from experience, starting a business involved enough risks that that option wasn't on my short list. (Full disclosure: At age 80 I did start a small publishing business, but thanks to almighty Amazon and its publishing platform, the financial risk was small).

A significant part of the reason Boomers start businesses is the financial incentive. Like everyone else, they have bills to pay. Finances weren't a problem for my dad, he had a pension to go along with his Social Security. That was all he and mom needed to live a comfortable life.

Pensions are a rarity for today's retirees however, unless their careers have been in the public sector. Meanwhile, in the absence of a pension, the combination of Social Security and income from a 401(k) just isn't enough, so many Boomers are electing to remain in the workforce and start businesses. Which accounts for the Kauffman Foundation's head-scratching statistic.

Here's another killer statistic that speaks volumes on the topic of Boomers choosing to remain in the workforce: today, a whopping 74 percent of people over 65 intend to keep working, up from a paltry 14 percent in 1995. The eye-opener in that statistic is the trend it represents: in 1995 one out of seven people continued working after 65, while today it's three out of four. That isn't a trend, it's an avalanche.

The reason behind that avalanche? It's primarily because a goodly portion of that 74 percent have no choice but to continue working thanks to another troubling statistic that says that the average American couple is going to incur $250,000 in hospital bills over and above what Medicare pays.

Yikes, the Golden Years ain't cheap.

Books have been written about what happens after our initial working career is finished. Check out Marc Freedman's *"The Big Shift"* if you want to read my favorite. One of Freedman's premises is that those of us who don't have pensions need a new roadmap of life. Instead of history's three stages (Learn. Earn. Retire), today we need a fourth stage. Freedman calls that fourth stage an Encore Career. (Learn. Earn. Encore career. THEN retire.) We're living too long these days, Freedman says—our life no longer fits the model our parents and grandparents used.

Here's the cool thing about how Encore careers work; besides the financial benefit they deliver, they can also help make aging gratifying, rewarding, and downright fun. For me, the best decade of my life was my 60s.

My second-best decade? My 70s.

I define the word "best" as "making the biggest difference in people's lives." That is what is fun for me, which is why I do it. Self-indulging, I suppose you'd call it, and you'd be right.

Steven Covey once wrote that for folks to live a fulfilling life, the Four Ls must be present. Covey's four Ls included . . .

- Live: A roof over our head, food on the table,
- Love: Someone, or something, to love,
- Learn: The unending pursuit of knowledge, and
- Leave a Legacy: Making a mark on the world.
- What if Covey's Leaving a Legacy became the endgame for millions of Americans following their working careers? Kind of a Peace Corps for Seniors. What kind of an impact would that have on our communities and our country?

Steven Jobs' stated mission in life was "to make a small dent in the universe." What if striving to make a small dent in the world took the place of retirement?

How many small dents would it take to make a big one?

MY WISDOM:

"If you want to be missed when you're finished, go

out with a bang, not a whimper."

Eight Decades in Nine Soundbites

"The things that get you fired when you're young are what get you lifetime achievement awards when you're old." —FRANCIS FORD COPPOLA

ONE OF MY FAVORITE MENTEES IS Kenzie, a smart, independent, and delightfully sassy Millennial. One of the many things I find intriguing about Kenzie is that she's eons ahead of her time when it comes to asking good questions. She'll smack you with a zinger right when you least expect it and then sit back and watch you struggle to come up with a cogent response.

Kenzie, like so many of her millennial counterparts, is also an incurable free spirit, I've been mentoring her for three years now and I'm never quite sure how long that will last; she could be gone to Morocco, Tanzania, or Iceland at the drop of a hat. I'd like to be her travel agent.

A year or so ago, I asked Kenzie to do some prep work for an upcoming mentoring session. The day before we were to meet, she emailed me that she hadn't completed her homework and needed to postpone our discussion on the related topic until the following meeting. In the meantime, however, she asked (well, she didn't *exactly* ask, which is one of the reasons I call her sassy) that I answer four questions at tomorrow's meeting. All as part of her learning experience, she explained.

So here we go, Kenzie's four questions . . .
Tell me about a time when you found your work to be most challenging.

- What brings you joy?
- What do you consider one of your biggest accomplishments and what challenges did you face achieving it?
- What is the number one lesson you learned from each decade of your life?

Lover of thought-provoking questions that I am, I gladly overlooked Kenzie's blowing off her assignment. I allowed her such dispensation because I thought the fourth question was so outstanding, it offset her turning the tables on me. In the course of answering that question I was treated to a 30,000-foot view of my life, a view I'd never taken the time to compile.

How can you top a question that does that?

So, in the interest of motivating you to ask yourself this same question, here, in nine condensed soundbites, are the lessons I learned from each of the eight decades I've been around. Hopefully, seven years from now, I'll have one more to add to the list.

The #1 Lesson I Learned from Each Decade of My Life

- **Age 0 to 10:** Sports are fun. You name the game and I played it.
- **Age 10-20:** I love to work. Thanks, Mom and Dad, for passing on that work ethic.
- **Age 20-30:** Mom was right . . . well, most of the time She was right about relationships, raising kids, careers, most of my friends, accountability, and staying busy.
- **Age 30-40:** I needed to be my own boss.
- **Age 40-50:** It's a tossup: (a) Marriage is not forever (what is?) and (b) Alcohol sucks. I've seen too many good people let alcohol mess up their life.

- **Age 50-60:** Writing gets better with age.
- **Age 60-70:** I can change lives.
- **Age 70-80:** The older we get, the wiser we get. People start to listen to us.
- **Age 80-90:** Too early to call, but writing and mentoring still fill my days.

So, there you have it. Thanks to Kenzie's reversing the tables on me, I've whittled my life down to less than 250 words.

Try it yourself. The older you are, the more meaningful the exercise becomes.

MY WISDOM:

"Our decades add up and tell the story of

who we've become."

Passing It On

"We make a living by what we get, we make a life by what we give." —WINSTON CHURCHILL

WHAT'S NEXT, WE WONDER, AS TIME marches on and our years pile up. We have now become elders (see modernelderacademy. com if you want to know the derivation of the term "elder"). How do we want to be spending our next week, month, or upcoming year? Even our next decade?

What will become of those thousands of hours we've spent doing things, experiencing things, and living our stories? And, what about that burgeoning stockpile of experiences we've accumulated, what will become of them? And how about all that hard-earned wisdom that is curdling in our brain, waiting to turn into cream?

The overarching question of them all, however, is once we arrive at that time in our life when we can do whatever we damn well please, what will become of all the wisdom we've earned?

Heaven knows we have plenty of options. The worst of those options is to waste it.

The best? Why of course. To share it.

We elders can share our wisdom by volunteering for a nonprofit. Even in tiny Bend, we have over 100 viable social-service nonprofits. Or we can help our city, county, or state governments serve their constituents better. We can help people in need, like Gretchen and Sue did at Walmart over the Christmas Holidays. Or, we don't have to wait until Christmas to do something that feels good: we can buy a stranger a cup of coffee any time of year, as my Hispanic friend did for me in Tucson. We can read to people who are just learning to read, we can befriend a kid in need of a caring adult, or we can deliver lunch to a housebound senior.

Or, we can do what Piglet did . . .

"Pooh," he whispered.

"Yes, Piglet?"

"Nothing," said Piglet, taking Pooh's paw. "I just wanted to be sure of you."

Piglet's choice was to be a caring friend for Pooh. We can never care too much for our friends.

While Piglet's choice is hard to beat (we can all use a friendly paw to hold), here's my personal favorite. We can be a teacher, a coach, and a friend, all wrapped into one.

Which is, to say, we can be a mentor. We can share our wisdom with the people we want to help.

The cool thing about mentoring is that it not only will benefit the person on the receiving end, it also will benefit us, the person on the giving end. Which means we'll still be learning new and interesting stuff at our old age, which brings me back to one of Steven Covey's four principles for leading a fulfilling life. Live, love, *learn,* and leave a legacy. Remember? Mentoring fulfills the learning principle.

Here's a sampling of just a few things we elders can learn while mentoring . . .

- We can learn from the people we mentor. If our mentee is a Millennial we can learn about technology and communication and what makes people in that age group tick.
- We can learn from ourselves. This happens to me all the time; I answer my mentee's question and then sit back and marvel at what I just said. "Wow!" I say to myself, "I didn't know I knew that!"

- We can feel younger by hanging around people who are younger than us. It's osmosis at work.
- We can make new friends. It's difficult to imagine a successful mentoring relationship where mentor and mentee don't end up as good friends. And who can't use more of those?
- I've learned and re-learned this lesson so many times: a successful mentoring relationship can be just as rewarding for the person doing the mentoring as it is for the person being mentored. It's a twofer.

No, wait, make that a threefer. Onefer the mentee, twofer the mentor, and threefer for the community where the two of us live.

MY WISDOM:

"Mentoring: taking the trial and error out of life."

The Lessons I Learned from Writing This Book

Charlie Brown: "We only live once, Snoopy."

Snoopy: "Wrong. We only die once. We live every day."
—CHARLES SCHULZ

STEPHEN KING, IN HIS BOOK "ON Writing," explains that there are two kinds of writers, those who prepare an outline and then follow it, and those who don't and then wing it. He goes on to say that those writers who wing it (I'm one) are as anxious to finish writing their book as their readers are to finish reading it. Both want to see how the book is going to end.

Lest I forget, in the case of nonfiction books, which this one is, we wing-it writers are also anxious to find out, once we've finished the book, what we've learned from writing it. Was our time spent worth the effort?

When I set out on this *Where Wisdom Comes From* journey, I had no idea what I'd learn from the process. But now that I'm finished, I can answer that question. Here are the top three lessons I've learned from the (largely enjoyable) nine months I've spent writing this book.

We're the product of our choices: Before we set foot on this earth, we didn't have the choice of selecting our parents, our gender, or how much hair we'd have on our head. However, once the cord was cut, our choices began to flow.

Today, we make dozens of choices every day, hundreds every week, and thousands every month. We make big choices, like who are friends will be, and little choices, like what to have for dinner, and in-between choices, like whether to fix the damn fridge or replace it.

Ultimately, we are the sum of the choices we make. The better the choices, the better the life.

We all need someone: We all need someone … someone to hold our hand, someone to believe in us, and, yes, someone to wag a finger in our face when we get lost. Someone to help us make life's journey better than it would have been on its own.

That someone could be a parent, grandparent, spouse, partner, friend, teacher, coach, mentor, even a neighbor. In the best case, that someone would enter our life in our early years, but whenever he or she comes along, later is better than not at all. It's never too late to learn.

It's all about Execution: My favorite business saying of all time came out of the lips of one Nolan Bushnell, the founder of Atari (remember their arcade games?). Bushnell, an inveterate entrepreneur, said *"anyone who can take a shower can have a good idea, what matters is what happens after you towel off."* It's easy to have ideas, Bushnell was saying, it's turning those ideas into something tangible that is the difficult part.

Some of my favorite people in the world are the "get shit doners." Those are the people who can make stuff, fix stuff, and execute stuff. Without them, we'd still be snacking on meat and water on Friday nights instead of pizza and beer.

So, thanks, dear reader, for staying with me this far. And how about you? You've taken two hours out of your life to read this book, two hours to explore a new way of thinking about where wisdom comes from. Two hours that you'll never get back.

What are the top three lessons you learned from those two hours? And how will you use what you've learned to make your world a better place to live?

MY WISDOM:

"We only get one chance. Why wouldn't we want

to make the best of it?"

Author's final note: If you want to share with me your top three lessons, I'd love to hear from you. Fire away. Jim.schell5@gmail.com